Happy Teacher

A Scientific Approach
to Being Happier in
the Classroom

Paul Murphy

Happy Teacher Copyright © 2017
by Paul Murphy

Table of Contents

Happiness Comes First

If you are fortunate, you teach at a school with lots of resources and students who get what they need at home. Your colleagues are cheerful people who smile often. Your principal is supportive and cares what you think. Your administration involves you in decisions. Your school has meaningful and reachable goals for students. When those goals are reached, teachers are recognized for their success. Your workload isn't overwhelming. Neither are the sizes of your classes. Your time is valued. The staff comes together to support each other in tough moments. The meetings you attend are engaging and relevant to your work. Your principal trusts you to do your job, but she'll stop by your room to see what kinds of things your students are learning and to offer guidance based on her personal experience and professional expertise. Professional development sessions are focused, and you leave feeling like you learned something that will make you a better teacher. Every morning, you and your colleagues wake up energized and excited to start another day of teaching. You can't wait for the bell to ring and your students to file enthusiastically into the room.

If you teach at a school like this, then I am both pleased and sorry for you. I am pleased because you likely have a fulfilling career as a teacher. You're probably already happy at work. I am sorry because you just wasted a few bucks buying this book.

Since you are reading this, the following may sound more familiar:

You are frequently stressed at work. There's too much to do and not enough time to do it. On top of that, you're forced to sit through useless meetings and PD sessions that do nothing to make you a better educator. You have a lot of students. Many of them need much more than you can provide. You do what you can, but you know it's not enough. Hell, sometimes you're just happy to get through the day with your job and sanity intact.

Your colleagues seem to be the same way, though no one wants to admit it. They're exhausted. Their smiles are forced. Many are overweight. A few seem depressed. They're either apathetic or flat-out cynical. Your principal isn't much help either. If he's not dutifully following orders from his own supervisors, he's trying to implement yet another new program on top of the ones you're already struggling to get off the ground. He micromanages but isn't clear about how you can improve. He's difficult to meet with because he's so busy, but not so busy that he can't fire off a fusillade of emails that require even more work from you.

Most mornings, you drag yourself out of bed and drive to school, lacking the enthusiasm you know you need to be an effective teacher. Still, you go. You show up. This is the job you wanted, after all. So you dig deep and put on a smile and do your best.

You don't get to escape on weekends or breaks either. You have to do all those things you didn't have time for during the workweek. You check papers, reply to emails, plan for tomorrow and next week, locate resources because those provided by your district aren't very good, brainstorm ideas for dealing with students who have behavior problems, send reminders to parents and students about everything from homework to permission slips to special events, engage with your personal learning network on social media, and read to stay on top of your profession.

When you do have success, it isn't happiness you feel but momentary relief. After all, you didn't succeed with *all* kids. You fret over those you didn't reach. You're told you should. *All children can learn*, you remind yourself. It was called No Child Left Behind, after all, not A Few Children Left Behind. You're told to differentiate so that all kids' needs are met, and yet you're handed one-size-fits-all programs that you're required to teach with fidelity. And even if you do your best and get results, you can be sure there will be another area in need of improvement. So you start all over again. New program. New goal. Same stress.

You want to be better. You want to be effective. Your job matters. You've been told many times that you're the most important in-school factor for student achievement. According to Eric Hanushek, your effectiveness contributes to how much money the kids in your class will eventually make.[1] By extension, you, along with your fellow educators, are directly affecting the future U.S. economy, which of course will greatly impact the world economy. Put simply, the future of the planet is in your hands. No pressure or anything.

It's been argued that everything people do, they do because they are seeking happiness. It need not be immediate happiness. You get on a treadmill not because you derive a feeling of instant gratification, but because you believe better health will lead to more happiness now and in the future. You believe that if you achieve, you will be happy. The more professional success you have, the more happiness you will feel. Why else would you work so hard?

But what if you have it backward? What if the opposite is actually true? What if success doesn't cause happiness, but being happy causes success? What if your lack of happiness at work is making it less likely that you will succeed?

There have been no shortages of accomplished, miserable people. Kurt Cobain, Ernest Hemingway, Alexander McQueen, Robin Williams, and David Foster Wallace are just a few of the many people who preferred death to what were seemingly very successful lives. Many other accomplished people died as a result of drugs they took to cope with depression and other mental health disorders. Clearly, success does not ensure contentment.

Conversely, there are plenty of unsuccessful people who don't seem at all bothered by their lack of accomplishment. A 2011 Gallup poll found that Latin Americans were the most positive people in the world. 85 percent of respondents in Panama and Paraguay answered yes to all five questions Gallup asked to determine people's happiness. Other countries in the top ten included El Salvador, Ecuador, Guatemala, and Costa Rica. The World Bank ranks Panama 54th in Gross Domestic Product per capita. Paraguay ranks 106th. On the other hand, a lowly 46 percent of respondents from Singapore, a nation with a GDP per capita that ranks them third in the world, answered all five questions affirmatively, ranking them last in positive emotions.[2] Clearly, happiness is not found by simply earning more money. It's also not found in Singapore.

It should not come as a surprise, then, that a review of 225 studies found that happiness doesn't always follow success. In fact, research shows the opposite: Happiness *causes* success. Sonja Lyubomirsky, Ph.D., of the University of California, Riverside, and colleagues reviewed three types of studies that asked questions like, "Are happy people more successful than unhappy people? Does happiness precede success? Does positive affect lead to success-oriented behaviors?"

The results suggest that happiness leads to greater success in life. Lyubomirsky says, "This may be because happy people frequently experience positive moods and these positive moods prompt them to be more likely to work actively toward new goals and build new resources. When people feel happy, they tend to feel confident, optimistic, and energetic, and others find them likable and sociable."[3]

If you're working like a dog under the assumption that you'll be happy when you achieve ultimate success, then you're wasting a lot of energy. As Neil Pasricha, author of *The Happiness Equation*, says, you should "be happy first."

So are you a happy teacher? If not, how can you become one? It is only after you've found happiness at work that you can expect to thrive in the classroom. That is what this book, and the science behind happiness, will help you do.

1. Are Teachers Happy?

Since success at work starts with employee happiness, and since a teacher's success directly impacts student learning, society has a vested interest in ensuring that teachers are happy at school. For the most part, it is failing.

First, the good news. Teachers are generally happy with their lives. The Gallup-Healthways Well-Being Index attempts to assess the satisfaction of people across different professions. In 2013, it interviewed nearly 10,000 American teachers and rated them in the areas of physical, emotional, and financial health. Teachers scored higher on this ranking than every profession except doctors.[4] Teachers, it seems, enjoy pretty happy lives.

Teachers tend to have a lot of positive daily experiences. Because children smile 400 times a day on average, adults often feel happier around them. 88 percent of teachers said they smiled or laughed the day before taking the survey, the highest of any profession.[5]

Teachers, like doctors, do not have to search for meaning in their work. That's one of the best parts of the job: We know that what we do matters, and having a purpose in life is related to higher levels of happiness.

But although teachers enjoy their lives, they like their jobs a whole lot less. Teachers did not score well when it came to questions about their work environment. Their answers placed them eighth out of 14 occupation groups. Teachers scored lower than miners, construction workers, and farmers.[6] That's right, *miners*, who work *underground* and get diseases with horrible names like *black lung*, enjoy their work environment more than teachers do. Maybe it's because miners are trusted to do their jobs. The nation's teachers ranked dead last in saying their supervisor "always creates an environment that is trusting and open."[7]

Teachers also reported very high stress, which is surprising because stress typically rises with income. Almost half of the surveyed teachers said they experienced stress every day, second only to doctors.[8] Evidently, teaching children is nearly as stressful as saving people's lives.

In 2012, the MetLife Survey of the American Teacher polled 1,000 teachers. It found a record decline in the percentage of teachers who said they were satisfied with their jobs. Teacher satisfaction in 2012 (the last year the survey was given) was at its lowest point in 25 years.[9]

The primary driver of teacher dissatisfaction is stress. In 1985, 36 percent of teachers reported they were under great stress at least several days a week. Today, that number is 51 percent. For elementary teachers, it's even higher at 59 percent. Those with low job satisfaction are more than twice as likely as those who are satisfied to feel under great stress several days a week.[10]

The Gallup-Healthways survey also revealed that only 31 percent of teachers were emotionally engaged at work.[11] The rest were either "not engaged" or "actively disengaged." That would probably describe the high school teacher I had who put a student in charge of running the film projector while he took naps at his desk.

11

Given all this, it's perhaps not surprising that 30 percent of teachers surveyed planned to leave the profession within five years, up from 17 percent in 2010. BBC News recently published an article with the headline "More than 50 percent of Teachers in England Plan to Quit in Next Two Years." Most cited heavy workloads as the reason. Two-thirds said teacher morale had fallen over the last five years.[12]

So what's causing all the stress and emotional detachment? Day-to-day experiences, rather than factors like years of experience or grades taught, made the most difference. Unhappier teachers were more likely to have had increases in class size and more students coming to class hungry. Their schools tended to serve needier families. How teachers were perceived by other professionals also mattered. Only about a third of teachers said they felt part of a valued profession.[13]

The moral seems to be that teachers are very happy people as long as they aren't actually teaching.

The disillusionment starts early. Several studies have estimated that between 40 and 50 percent of new teachers leave within their first five years. One in ten don't even finish their first year in the classroom.[14] The National Commission on Teaching and America's Future reports an annual turnover rate of 15.7 percent compared to 11.9 percent for other fields. They also report that four out of every ten students who pursue undergraduate degrees in teaching never enter a classroom at all.[15]

Just a short time ago, college students were willing to give teaching a try, only to quickly discover that it wasn't for them. Now, fewer are considering the profession at all. According to a 2016 report from the Learning Policy Institute, enrollment in teacher preparation programs fell 35 percent from 2009 to 2014. The problem is especially bad in California, where enrollment in such programs declined by 53 percent from 2010 to 2015.[16]

There are 24 hours in a day. If you sleep for eight of them, that leaves 16 hours of awake time. Factoring in a half-hour commute each way (the U.S. average is 25 minutes) and seven hours at school, you're left with eight hours for yourself each day. This means that one-third of each workday is spent at school during the hours of the day when the sun is shining and all of your favorite places are open. We spend the most valuable hours of every workday at school. What a shame it is when those hours are spent in misery. What a sad waste of the best hours of our lives.

You cannot allow it to be this way. And I do mean *you*. Society does not seem eager to make the lives of teachers less stressful. While we would all appreciate more respect, more resources, more trust, and more involved parents and students, we cannot sit around waiting for others to improve our situations. As a poster in my classroom says, "Nobody is in charge of your happiness except you."

It is time to solve your own problem. Science has a lot to say about how to be happy. The remainder of this book will show you how to apply this science in your classroom so that you can enjoy work, come home with more energy, and be the happiest teacher — and person — you can possibly be.

2. What Makes Teachers Unhappy

Before we learn what science has to say about happiness, we should first understand what makes teachers unhappy. After all, one simple way to improve our happiness is to remove the things from our lives that make us miserable. Different surveys have concluded that a variety factors contribute to low teacher job satisfaction. But when looked at as a whole, it becomes clear that there is one major culprit: stress.

Stress can be defined as having to face a challenge while feeling you have too few resources to meet that challenge. Most of the things that make teachers unhappy fall under this definition.

Teachers with low job satisfaction are more than twice as likely as those who say they are very satisfied with their job to feel under great stress several days a week. In addition, unhappy teachers are more likely to teach in schools where two-thirds or more of students come from low-income families. The same survey found that teacher happiness falls when a majority of students are behind in language arts and math.[17]

So one way to improve your happiness is to teach in a district where parents earn a middle class income and students don't struggle academically. Teachers seem to understand this. Studies consistently show that teachers who are better trained, have more experience, and are licensed in the subjects they teach are more likely to teach in affluent schools. The same is true for National Board Certified teachers.[18]

In other words, the most qualified teachers tend to choose to work in schools where they will experience less stress on the job.

Many teachers are even willing to accept lower pay for better-prepared students. Several years ago, South Carolina offered an extra $18,000 to teachers willing to work in the state's weakest schools. The program attracted just 100 out of the 500 teachers it needed. Interviews with teachers revealed that they listed location, lack of administrative support, poor working conditions, and a lack of preparation for reasons they didn't apply.[19] The same preferences explain why many teachers accept lower pay to work in private schools. These teachers know that more money isn't enough to compensate for the added stress.

Most studies have found little correlation between class size and stress. What matters is the type of students in the room. Low-performing students and those with behavior problems cause teacher dissatisfaction. If you're skeptical, try the following thought experiment: Think of the five most challenging students in your grade level. Option one requires you to take all five of those students and ten others of your choice, giving you 15 total students. Option two allows you to choose every one of your entire class of 30 students. While there are some teachers — those who embrace hard cases and look forward to helping the neediest kids — who might take the first option, the research shows that most teachers will choose door number two, even if there's a financial incentive to not do so.

Budget cuts are also associated with lower morale and greater stress. Teachers at schools where budgets decreased within the past year were less likely than those at other schools to be very happy with their profession.[20] Of course, these cuts often happen at schools where stress is already high, compounding the problem.

Teachers, like people in every job, want their bosses to trust them and value their input. In a 1986 survey, all principals agreed that they should recognize and develop teachers' leadership abilities by involving them in decision making. 96 percent of principals reported that they did so at the time. Nearly all teachers supported this effort, but only seven in ten said this was actually occurring in their schools.

The use of email can also raise teachers' stress by affecting their emotions. Because emails lack the cues we use to interpret people's words in face-to-face conversation, we often interpret them negatively. It's what makes playful sarcasm so risky in textual form. If you check your email regularly throughout the day, you may experience a lot of stress.

Think about how many emails you get at work. Every time you check them, there's a chance you'll respond emotionally, often negatively, and many times without good reason. In his book, *The Happiness Equation*, author Neil Pasricha tells a story about working for a powerful and well-respected CEO who never replied to his emails. When Pasricha finally worked up the courage to ask the CEO why he never responded, Pasricha received the following advice:

"Neil," the businessman said, "there's a problem with email. After you send one, the responsibility of it goes away from you and becomes the responsibility of the other person. It's a hot potato. An email is work given to you by somebody else."[21]

Check your work email right now to see if it's true. How many of your last ten emails require something — an action, more work, a response — from you? I just checked mine. Here are the summarized contents of my ten most recent emails:

1. Information about the upcoming week (no action required)

2. A request from a student to share a document with her (work for me)

3. A request that I fill out a survey (work for me)

4. One from the principal telling me to set up my parent-teacher conference schedule and email it out to parents by Monday (work for me)

5. A link to a T-shirt order form for March is Reading Month (work for me if I want the shirt, which I don't)

6. A request that I preview some material ahead of a meeting next week (work for me)

7. A reminder to get my progress monitoring done so I can have my name entered into a weekly drawing (work for me)

8. A request to look over a schedule to see if it works (work for me)

9. A short email providing information (no action required)

10. Details about March is Reading Month (eventual work for me)

One simple way to reduce stress at work is to regulate how often and when you check your email. I used to check it all the time on my phone, which was always in my pocket. Now I leave the phone on my desk and only check it in the morning before students arrive, during lunch, and again before leaving at the end of the day.

When stress becomes chronic and overwhelming, teachers burn out. Human service professionals are especially prone to burnout, with teachers have the highest burnout rate of any public service job in the U.S.[22] It probably won't take you long to think of a burned out teacher who has either quit or seems on the verge of doing so.

In a recent large-scale study, California teachers reported three major reasons for leaving teaching: an inadequate system, bureaucratic impediments, and a lack of collegial support. Specifically, these former teachers cited poor professional development, a lack of textbooks, too little time to prepare lessons, excessive paperwork, unnecessary classroom interruptions, and too many restrictions from administrators and policymakers on how they were to teach. They also said that they did not have "a strong team" to draw on at their school, and that there was too little trust and respect among the staff.[23]

Teachers are stressed out, and for lots of reasons. This stress is destroying their happiness at work and causing them to emotionally detach or quit altogether. To be successful, teachers first need to be happy in the classroom. But how? The answers might surprise you, because the things we think will make us happy often don't.

3. Predicting Our Own Happiness

In his book *Stumbling on Happiness*, Harvard social psychologist Daniel Gilbert discusses our ability to accurately predict how we will feel in the future. He calls this "affective forecasting" and concludes that we make a lot of mistakes. When thinking about our futures we focus on certain details and neglect other equally important ones. We overestimate the intensity and duration of how we will feel about both positive and negative events. We allow our present emotional states to influence how we think we will feel in the future. We rely on faulty memories to color how we think about future occurrences. We misremember how we used to feel about things. We fail to take our own personalities into account when we consider how we will feel about an imagined event.

In short, what we think will make us happy often doesn't, and what we think will ruin us often turns out to have far less impact than we feared.

Our expectations greatly impact our happiness. If we're told by our friends that we just have to see a certain movie, and if we read reviews about how great the movie is, and if the movie has already made a pile of money, then we expect to like the movie a lot. If the movie falls even a little short of our lofty expectations, we will dislike it much more than if we had gone into it without any expectations at all.

Restaurants understand this. How many times have you entered a busy restaurant and seen a large group of people

19

waiting for a table? You think to yourself, *Boy, this is going to be a long wait.* You start mentally estimating how long the wait might be. *Why, I bet it's going to be an hour.* Maybe you should go somewhere else, you think. You'll just ask the hostess and see what she says. When you ask and are told the wait will be 40 minutes, you decide to stay, since it was less than you assumed. Then, 25 minutes later, the little electronic thing you're holding onto happily buzzes and lights up, and you feel like you've won something. The restaurant has exceeded your expectations. As a result, you are much happier than you would have been had someone told you before you left the house that you'd have to wait 25 minutes to get seated.

Unfortunately, many of us have experienced the opposite of this as well. We walk right in, sit right down, order quickly, and then, 20 minutes later, we still don't have our appetizer. Now, even though it's been five minutes less than the previous example, we start to wonder what's taking so long. Our happy feelings have disappeared. We question whether we ever want to come back. We consider leaving a scathing review online. How long can it take to deep-fry some cheese?

Teachers aren't immune to the damaging effects of having high expectations. Many college students and new teachers expect teaching to be something it isn't. Their imaginations take what they think they know — a limited view of the job they've cobbled together from TV, conventional wisdom, movies, touching stories shared over social media, and their own experiences as students — to create an expectation of the job that doesn't reflect reality. It is my belief that so many young teachers leave the profession as a result of their flawed imaginations. They realize quite early in their careers that teaching is far different from the job they expected it to be.

If college students really want to know what the job is like, they should ask real teachers. But if your college experience was anything like mine, there were few opportunities to do so. When you did, the veteran teachers, perhaps not wanting to pop your bubbly enthusiasm and recognizing the importance of bringing in new blood, often sugar-coated their narratives. They told you what you already knew — that the job can be extremely rewarding, that they're doing work that makes a difference, that they love working with kids. They left out the stuff that only shows up in anonymous surveys: the stress, the dwindling resources, administrative micromanagement, mind-numbing meetings, the indifference of some parents, and everything else that, if shared, would have given aspiring teachers a more honest accounting of the job.

But even if prospective teachers were provided the opportunity to ask teachers what teaching is really like, and even if teachers were brutally honest, research shows that the college kids wouldn't listen.

Gilbert describes three experiments that prove the best way to predict our future feelings about an event is to rely on the reports of people who have recently experienced such an event. He says, "This trio of studies suggests that when people are deprived of the information that imagination requires and are thus forced to use others as surrogates, they make remarkably accurate predictions about their future feelings, which suggests that the best way to predict our feelings tomorrow is to see how others are feeling today."[24] But when a new group of participants in those same studies were told about the findings of the prior studies and then asked whether they wanted to rely on their own predictions or on a report of a randomly selected individual who had already gone through the experiment, almost every volunteer chose to rely on their own faulty imaginations.

The reason, says Gilbert, is that we tend to think we're unique, and that just because someone else feels a certain way about a set of circumstances does not mean that we will. But Gilbert asserts that we are wrong to think this way. While we spend more time noticing the differences among individuals, the reality is that humans are far more alike than different, and not only biologically. People's emotional responses are far less varied than we assume. So while the best way to predict your future feelings is to ask someone who is currently doing the very thing you're thinking about doing, we don't, because, as Gilbert writes, "We don't realize just how similar we all are, [so] we reject this reliable method and rely instead on our imaginations, as flawed and fallible as they may be."[25]

It's not just young people who are fooled by their imaginations. Veteran teachers are equally susceptible. While these teachers possess all the facts and understand the sometimes grim realities of the job, many of them engage in "I'd be happy if" scenarios.

They say to themselves, "I'd be happy if I had a different principal. I'd be happy if I had better students. I'd be happy if parents were more involved. I'd be happy if I was paid more money and got more respect from society. I'd be happy if I had more time to plan."

The problem is that we aren't very good at these kinds of affective forecasts. What we think will make us happy often won't. And when it does, that happiness will last for a shorter time and with less intensity than we imagined.

The other argument against "I'd be happy if" fantasies has to do with what psychologists call "hedonic adaptation." This is our tendency to quickly become used to pretty much anything. It's why your brand new house won't generate as much pleasure in a year as it does now, and why the big screen TV you were so excited to purchase becomes just another TV within a few months.

I experience hedonic adaptation every time I travel West. I live in Michigan, but I've made a handful of trips to the mountainous western U.S. One summer, my family visited nine different national parks. At the start of the trip, we'd point out every mountain peak in the distance to our daughter. We oohed and aahed at the landscape and imagined how amazing it would be to live among such beautiful scenery. We said things like, "Oh, can you imagine waking up every morning and seeing that out your back window?"

I'm sure you know what happened. By the end of the trip, I barely noticed the mountains anymore, and I certainly wasn't awed by their majesty. My daughter kept her nose in her Percy Jackson novel while I complained about what the peaks and valleys were doing to my brakes and gas mileage.

But what do most of us do after we've adapted to and become bored with what we have? We decide that the antidote to our waning enthusiasm is *more*! We tell ourselves that we must have been wrong. It wasn't the new job we wanted. It was the new job *and* a much bigger salary! The new car didn't lead to lasting happiness, but a new boat will! We just didn't dream big enough! We choose a new, bigger goal, and we're off again!

The truth is we were wrong, but not about our goals and aspirations. We were wrong about what makes us happy in the first place.

Perhaps the most extreme example of hedonic adaptation is lottery winners. Most of us dream of winning the lottery. We imagine all the problems that kind of money would solve. We fantasize about giving enough to our parents so they can retire, or funding our nieces' and nephews' college educations. We imagine vacation houses and sports cars. Surely, if we win the lottery, we tell ourselves, *then* we will be happy for the rest of our lives.

Not so. First, money does, to a certain extent, buy happiness. Having enough money to pull yourself out of poverty and into the middle class will certainly improve your happiness. But Nobel Prize-winning economist Daniel Kahneman and Princeton economist Angus Deaton found that income only makes a significant impact on daily happiness when earning up to $75,000 annually. After that, more money does not make much of a difference.[26] A famous 1978 study of Illinois lottery winners found that, within a year, the winners weren't any happier than the losers.[27]

We're not just wrong about money and material possessions making us happy. Research has also found that:

- Better-educated people are not happier.[28]
- Older people are happier than younger people.[29]
- We're not actually happier when we spend time with our kids.[30]
- Achieving our goals does not lead to the lasting happiness we expect it to.

Think about why you work and why you want to be good at it. Your belief is:

1. Work hard
2. Achieve success
3. Be happy

But that's wrong. Research shows that your belief should be:

1. Be happy
2. Work hard
3. Achieve success

The beauty of this belief is that you don't really need number three. Success is great, but if you're already happy, do you need it? Will it destroy your life if you don't achieve your professional ambitions? Not if you're already happy.

The grass over there isn't greener. Stop thinking you'd be happy if only things were different. Don't expect success at work to lead to lasting happiness. If you want to know how you are likely to feel about something, ask someone who has recently done that thing. Put happiness first.

4. Choose Your Attitude

Are you even capable of happiness? It's a question you might be wondering. After all, we're all wired differently. Some people seem born with the ability to sing, dance, perform complex computations, or shoot a basketball. We mortals might practice our tails off, but our stubby bodies will never allow us to be the next Michael Phelps. Our nasally voices guarantee we won't be getting a paycheck for voiceover work. Why should happiness be any different? Aren't some people just naturally happier than others, regardless of their circumstances? How much control do we really have over our own happiness, and how much is genetically encoded in our DNA?

Most teachers I know have faced the following situation: They have a student who is really struggling in math. He does things the teacher can't even begin to understand. His number sense seems to come from some place where the rules of the universe are opposite our own. Story problems? Forget about it. The teacher meets with his mother to discuss his concerns, and the mother says something like, "Oh, math. Well, I was never very good at math, either. He probably gets that from me."

Is this an excuse you accept?

Of course not! We teachers believe that the students in front of us are not destined to their parents' fates. We believe they are their own people and that they can develop new skills with good instruction and lots of practice. Why would you not believe the same thing about happiness?

But in case you're a skeptic, a number of twin and adoption studies have led scientists to conclude that approximately 50 percent of overall well-being is hereditary. Another 10 percent is what happens to you. The other 40 percent is within your control.

Again, 40 percent of your happiness is up to you!

It's similar to the kid whose mom stinks at math. He probably won't be the next John Nash, but he's not a lost cause.
Neither are you. You can greatly enhance your happiness through intentional activities and practice. It starts by recognizing that you have control over your thoughts.

You might think that's ridiculous. How else would you have thoughts if you didn't decide to have them? If you don't control your thoughts, then how in the world do they get in there? Of course you have control over your thoughts!

But do you really?

The other day I was driving to work. I was running a little behind, and I had a lot of things to do before the students entered the classroom. Because I don't have a break until lunch, there was no time to get these things done except before the morning bell. I was making a mental checklist of all my tasks, doing it quite intentionally, when I came upon a garbage truck moving at a glacial pace.

My route to work is over rural roads that undulate like a sound wave, so I knew I was likely stuck driving 30 miles per hour and stopping every few hundred yards while more trash was fed into the gaping back end of the truck.

I pounded my steering wheel and audibly cursed my awful luck. I swore loudly at the private company that decided collecting trash on a Tuesday in the middle of the work commute was a good idea. I darted left to see if there was an opening large enough to allow me to pass. I shouted, actually shouted out loud, at the driver of the garbage truck, who was doing nothing except his thankless job.

By the time the garbage truck turned out of my way, my heart was racing, I was clenching my teeth, and my good mood was destroyed. I drove faster than I should have, and was probably more reckless than I ought to have been, in the hopes of regaining the lost time. It took me ten minutes to calm back down.

Did I have control over my thoughts? Technically, I suppose I did, but I can tell you I didn't make a conscious decision to become frustrated. Logically, my reaction made no sense. There was nothing I could do about the garbage truck's presence, its speed, its frequent stops, the terrain of the road, or the steady stream of oncoming traffic that prevented me from passing.

My anger did not make anything better. In fact, it made it worse. My state of mind could have caused even more problems. My increased speed could have resulted in being pulled over and made even more tardy. I could have caused an accident.

I wasn't really in control of my thoughts, because if I had been, I would have realized that those thoughts provided no benefit to me and made my life, at least for those fifteen or twenty minutes, demonstrably worse.

We all have moments like these. Moments where our thoughts betray us and lead us to make decisions we later regret. Moments where we retrospectively ask ourselves, "What the hell was I *thinking*?" We don't have nearly as much control over our thoughts as we think we do.

In 2008, the writer David Foster Wallace (*Infinite Jest*) gave a commencement address to the graduating class of Kenyon College. Among many pearls of wisdom, he said:

Learning how to think really means learning how to exercise some control over how and what you think. It means being conscious and aware enough to choose what you pay attention to and to choose how you construct meaning from experience. Because if you cannot exercise this kind of choice in adult life, you will be totally hosed. Think of the old cliché about 'the mind being an excellent servant but a terrible master.'

This, like many clichés, so lame and unexciting on the surface, actually expresses a great and terrible truth. It is not the least bit coincidental that adults who commit suicide with firearms almost always shoot themselves in: the head. They shoot the terrible master. And the truth is that most of these suicides are actually dead long before they pull the trigger.[31]

The first line above says it all:

Learning how to think really means learning how to exercise some control over <u>how</u> and <u>what</u> you think.

29

So choose wisely. Choose to appreciate what you have. Stop aspiring to greater heights in the hopes that new accomplishments will make you happier. Focus on life's small pleasures instead of expecting too much from big changes and events. Recognize that you will be fed up on occasion and realize that other people go through that too.

Here's a trick I use. I sometimes intentionally recall what it was like when I was a broke first-year teacher. This is actually somewhat challenging to do, as our mind plays tricks with our memories. We only remember some details. Our brains fill in others. Our present tends to influence how we perceive our past. But nevertheless, I try to conjure an accurate representation of my early teaching years. I remember how often I used to be observed by administrators who didn't trust me. I recall that horrible student I had in year three and how I didn't have the skills to manage him. I think back to the size of my early paychecks. Then I compare my younger self to my more experienced, more skilled, more trusted, and more financially secure present self. It helps put things into perspective.

As we stay longer at our jobs, our expectations rise. The job becomes an entitlement. We deserve everything we get and feel like we should be getting more. It's why older teachers are almost always more cynical than younger ones, even though, objectively, the older teachers are in much better positions. Those higher expectations mean disappointment stings more than it did when we were fresh out of college. We get angrier, become righteously indignant, and work ourselves into a frothy, emotional lather that harms our happiness when things don't go our way.

Our emotions affect everything we do and how we perceive our circumstances. What we think about and how we think about things makes the difference between enjoyment and misery. How you choose to think about your job, your school, your boss, your students, your students' parents, and daily occurrences largely determines how happy you will be in life and at work. Attitude, far more than circumstance, explains why a teacher in one room always seems to have a spring in her step and a smile on her face, while the grump across the hallway won't even say hello to his colleagues.

A month ago, my family had a spring break vacation planned for St. Louis. We were going to leave on a Saturday morning, arrive in time to see a magic show that night, then go to Six Flags on Sunday. Everything was packed and ready to go. We were all excited. Then my daughter started throwing up at two o'clock in the morning and continued to do so every thirty minutes, all through the night.

She couldn't spend seven hours in a car like that, so we called the hotel and rescheduled the trip for the second half of the week. There was nothing we could do about the magic show tickets. They were non-refundable and non-transferable. My daughter was bummed because her grandma and grandpa were also traveling to St. Louis the first half of the week and now we would miss them.

I had a choice about how to react to all of this. I could, as David Foster Wallace advised, decide *what* and *how* to think.

Partly because I didn't want my daughter to feel any worse than she already did, and partly because I had been researching and writing this book, I chose to find the silver linings in what was an unavoidable circumstance. The weather

31

for the rescheduled Six Flags day looked warmer and sunnier than the original date. Changing the hotel dates was less of a hassle than I expected it to be. I'd now be able to watch the semifinal games of the NCAA basketball tournament at home, whereas the original plan had me watching a magic show smack in the middle of the action. We could relax at home for a few days before hitting the road. Our friends would now be able to feed our cat instead of having the neighbors do it. I was still disappointed (those magic show tickets weren't cheap), but my attitude was much better than it would have been had I not exercised intentional control over what and how I thought.

We can't always control our emotions — stupid drivers piss us off, our best laid plans are ruined by unpredictable things like stomach bugs, the airline loses our luggage — but we can control our reactions to them. Or, as a poster hung on my classroom door says, "You are responsible for your actions no matter how you feel." I tell my students every year, "You can feel any way you want to. You won't get in trouble in my class for your emotions. But you have total control over how you act. And I will hold you accountable for your choices."

Being a happy teacher is a choice each of us can make. But choosing happiness doesn't mean we always feel happy. We don't deny our emotions. But we do realize we have control over what we do about them. It means we choose what to think about and how to think about it.

Part of having a positive attitude is simply noticing the many positive things that happen to you every single day. While many people believe that the way to happiness is to acquire the best stuff and have the greatest experiences, research has found that it is the frequency of positive events that matters more than their intensity.[32] Many days filled with small pleasures, like eating a favorite food, spending time with a valued friend, receiving a genuine compliment from a person you respect, and having a small success in the classroom, will lead to more enduring happiness than a European vacation. If you want to maintain happiness over the long haul, spend your money on bite-sized sources of happiness instead of big-ticket items, and train yourself to exercise control over your thoughts.

5. Be Nice

Doctors famously pledge to, "First, do no harm." If teachers were required to take a similar oath, I would recommend, "First, don't be a jerk."

Most people think they're nice. In one study, 98 percent of respondents said they were in the nicest 50 percent of the population, which of course is statistically impossible.[33] If you ask teachers if they're nice to their students, nearly all of them will assure you that they are. But if you spent a day in their classrooms, would you agree?

I'm not so sure. I've worked with a lot of teachers in my seventeen years as an educator. I'd classify most of them as "nice." However, if we apply the Golden Rule standard, how many would consistently pass?

The Golden Rule simply says that you should treat others how you would like to be treated. We teachers are very familiar with it; many of us remind our students of this basic standard of decency quite often. But some of us, including me, are at least occasionally hypocrites.

Teachers sometimes forget that children are people too.

Students don't find sarcastic remarks at their expense remotely amusing. They don't appreciate snide comments. They feel disrespected when their ideas are dismissed. They don't like being bossed around. They'd prefer a "please" at the end of requests. They like to hear "thank you" when they've done you a favor. They'd rather be smiled at than frowned at. They don't like being lectured to. They despise being embarrassed and chastised in front of their peers. They don't like being ignored.

Many adults talk to children in ways they would never think of talking to other adults. Some of it is the nature of our jobs; we have to authoritatively provide direction and correct poor choices. But other times it's simply because we can. Our harsh words can stem from frustration, but usually, it's about power. When teachers bully, demean, lecture, shout at, or otherwise disrespect their students, they're sending students a very simple message: I'm more powerful than you, so I can treat you how I want, and there's nothing you can do about it. Most of us are guilty of falling victim to this power play at times, so to avoid it, I remind myself of three things:

1. Don't say things to students I wouldn't want my principal to say to me during a staff meeting.

When I have a one-on-one meeting with my principal, I don't worry too much about how I phrase things. If asked for my honest opinion, I give it. If I think my principal is wrong about something, I will say so.

I expect my principal to do the same with me. In a one-on-one meeting, I want honesty from my principal. If he thinks I'm doing something wrong or could be doing something better, he should tell me. If he thinks I have a weakness, he has an obligation as my boss to inform me and give me pointers or direct me to resources that will help me improve. My rationale is that we're both adults, we're both professionals, we're both trying our best, but we're both human and will, on occasion, fall short or screw up. I'm a big boy, and I can take the criticism. He's the boss, so he better be able to take some too.

A staff meeting is a totally different animal because it is public. I rarely challenge or even disagree with my principal in a staff meeting. If I do, I choose my words very carefully and usually try to give my principal an out by saying something like, "I know this isn't coming from you, but has administration considered…"

There are a number of reasons you should not criticize your principal in front of the entire staff, but for the purposes of this chapter, I don't do it because I don't want him to do it to me. When your boss criticizes you publicly, you feel attacked. You feel ashamed and you become defensive. Your body triggers the fight-or-flight response because the brain is shouting, "DANGER! DANGER!" You either sit there and take it, fuming on the inside and plotting elaborate ways to get revenge, or you defend yourself vigorously and say something you'll regret later. Either way, you'll feel resentment toward your principal. You won't be doing that jerk any favors any time soon! You'll complain about him to your colleagues. The next time you disagree with him, maybe you won't be so respectful; he certainly didn't show you the same courtesy. You might even seek to undermine him at the next opportunity.

Students are humans too. They feel the same things you do. When you embarrass them in front of their peers by publicly scolding them, it's no different than your principal doing the same to you. In fact, students likely feel shame and resentment more acutely than you do because they're at an age when friendships matter more than just about anything. They care more about their classmates' opinion of them than you care about your colleagues' opinion of you. Good luck getting that student back on your side any time soon. You might be in for a very long year.

Instead of belittling students in front of their peers, talk to them privately about your concerns, just as you would want your principal to do to you.

2. Don't say things to students I wouldn't say to adults.

Any teacher who has attended more than a couple of professional development sessions knows that many teachers make horrible students. I've been to countless trainings where a group of teachers behave in a way they would never accept in their own classrooms. They talk during presentations, have off-topic side conversations, miss directions, check papers, work or play on their electronic devices, and don't respond to reasonable requests to bring their attention back to where it's supposed to be. It drives me crazy, and I've often had the urge to shush them, or worse.

But I don't.

I don't because that's not how adults interact with other adults. In fact, were I to tell a group of disrespectful teachers to be quiet and pay attention, I would suddenly be viewed as the disrespectful one. You're not supposed to snap at or boss around other grown-ups, even when they deserve it.

And yet many teachers seem to have no problem doing it to students. If we don't like it when our principal brusquely tells us to end our sidebar conversations and pull our attention back, then why do we think it's okay to do that to our students? If we prefer a kinder, gentler approach to regaining attention, then why don't we use a kinder, gentler approach to redirecting students? The rule I try to follow is: If I wouldn't say it to an adult who should be mature enough to handle it, why say it to a child who probably isn't?

3. Smile

Anyone who knows me knows I don't walk around with a smile on my face all day. My natural resting face is neutral at best and a scowl at worst. I used to have a coworker who would see me before school and ask if I was okay or tell me to smile. I would have to assure her that I was fine and not particularly unhappy. It's just how I look. It takes a lot to get a genuine smile out of me.

But when students enter my classroom in the morning, I smile at them. I try to smile throughout the day. Smiling is what nice people do. I envy my wife, who smiles easily and naturally, but not everyone is like that. For me, it takes a conscious effort, but that's no excuse to not do it. A lot of teaching is making conscious choices to do things that don't come naturally. Since I care about how students perceive me and because I know that being a pleasant person leads to many benefits, I smile.

Research shows that it takes five positive remarks to compensate for a single negative one. It takes three positive experiences to make up for a bad one. If you are mean to a student, it will take a lot of work to repair the relationship. When I am sarcastic or rude, I damage the relationship I have with not only the student on the receiving end but also with the entire class. Why?

Think about a time when a colleague has been treated shabbily by an administrator. Even though you may have a perfectly good relationship with that administrator, her treatment of your colleague affects your opinion of her. You wonder about her impartiality. Is she playing favorites? What if you're suddenly not a favorite? Will she treat you that way too? Why doesn't she understand that teachers talk and that her poor treatment of one teacher affects how the entire staff perceives her leadership? It comes down to one question that we're always asking about the people in our lives: Can I trust this person?

Students ask this too.

One way to gain trust is to be nice. In his book, *The Happy Teacher Habits,* California teacher Michael Linsin calls it being "consistently pleasant." He says, "By having a friendly disposition, your students will be naturally and irresistibly drawn to you — even, or especially, the most challenging among them."[34]

The reason for this is what social psychologists call the Law of Reciprocity, which simply means that when someone gives you something, you feel an obligation to give them something in return. It's why companies send you free address labels out of the blue and why car salesmen offer you a beverage. When you accept their gift, you immediately feel obliged to do something for them in return, like buy an extended warranty you'll never use.

Most winters, my family spends Presidents' Day weekend in Traverse City, Michigan, the "Cherry Capital of the World." One year, we visited a downtown store that sold cherry-themed items at inflated prices. There were small stations set up throughout the store. Each station had cherry flavored foods you could sample for free. There was cherry salsa and cherry flavored cheese spread, chocolate-covered cherries, and pretzel sticks that you could dip into — you guessed it — cherry mustard. The stations were arranged so that as you walked through the store you couldn't help but pass them.

The owners of the store understand the Law of Reciprocity. They know that a lot of tourists walk through their store. They also know that hardly any of them need their products and that their merchandise is overpriced. But by the time you've stopped at eight stations and eaten enough samples that you don't really need lunch for another couple of hours, the Law of Reciprocity is working overtime. You'll feel extremely guilty walking out of that store without buying something.

The Law of Reciprocity also applies to human interactions. It's hard to be a jerk to someone who is unfailingly nice to you. Most years, I read the children's novel *There's a Boy in the Girls' Bathroom* to my students. It tells the story of Bradley Chalkers, a bully who, with the help of his school counselor, is able to make friends and turn around his life. There's a scene in the story where Bradley's former friend Jeff is encouraged by his new friends to beat up Bradley. As they stand there looking at each other and the gang of kids eggs Jeff on, Bradley holds out his hand and says, "Hi, Jeff." And Jeff responds by saying "Hi, Bradley," and all the tension of the moment deflates like air from a popped balloon. I always joke afterward with the students that it's really hard to punch someone in the face after they've just smiled at you and said hi.

When you are nice to students, when you are *consistently pleasant*, it becomes very hard for students to stay angry at you. Most of us, and this includes kids, just don't have it in us to continue to be jerks to people who are always kind to us.

Being nice will also gain you leverage. We've all had the experience of having a new student join our class midway through the year. My district is located in the county seat, where a number of social services are available. Many new students come from transient families and lack the skills to succeed. Some have chips on their shoulders and can become behavior problems. But if you've spent the year being nice to your students, and they've responded as expected because of the Law of Reciprocity, then the new student will have a very hard time swimming against the current of your pleasant and respectful classroom culture.

The biggest reason to be nice to students, and the most relevant to this book, is that it will make you happier. How do you feel at the end of a long day of snapping at and scolding your students? How do you feel about yourself when you embarrass a student in front of her peers? Powerful? Probably. Justified? Perhaps. But I bet you don't feel proud of yourself, and I bet you don't feel very happy. I imagine you go home feeling pretty cruddy on those days. I've been there, and it's an exhausting place to be.

It's hard to feel happy when you act like a jerk. Being nice makes you more happy. Being nice when others would not be can further boost your self-image. We all tell ourselves stories about ourselves. We feel happier when those stories highlight the positive traits of our personalities. Scientists speculate that the reason why giving boosts happiness is because after we give, we see ourselves as the kind of person who gives, and we like thinking of ourselves in this positive way. When you are nice to a student who doesn't deserve it, that becomes a part of the story you tell yourself about you. You are a person who, even when treated poorly, responds with equanimity. You keep your cool, but even more than that, you respond the opposite of how weaker people respond. Your kindness is a strength.

A LEGACY OF BENEFITS

Being nice will help you with the management of your classroom, which will increase your happiness because you'll feel more competent at work and your students will accomplish more. You'll also leave work with more energy because you won't be emotionally dealing with behavior problems all day. And when you're nice, you'll create a legacy that can keep your happiness going year after year.

When you are consistently nice to your students, they will label you a nice teacher. If your colleagues fail in this area, you may be labeled *The* nice teacher. Don't discount this.

A lot of teachers say they'd rather be respected than liked, but they misunderstand: You don't have to be one or the other.

When you are The Nice Teacher, students will talk positively about you to their parents. Parents will then believe you *are* nice, based on nothing except the reports of their kids. Look at this from a parent's perspective. What do you want more than anything from your child's teacher? Some want teachers who challenge their kids. Some want content experts. Others want a master classroom manager. I want my kid to come home liking school so that she wants to go back day after day, year after year. I want her to associate learning with fun because we like things that are fun, and are more likely to keep doing those things. The biggest factor in whether my kid enjoys school is how her teacher treats her and the other kids in the room. There are very few parents who don't want a nice teacher for their kids.

When parents view you as someone who is nice, many will want their children in your room. Some will request you for their child's teacher. Parents who show this much interest and take the initiative to submit a teacher request form tend to be involved in other ways in their children's lives, and kids whose parents are invested in their educations tend to be pretty good students who are held to high expectations.

You'll also benefit from people's tendency to act consistently. You will have to mess up quite a lot for a parent who requested you to change his or her feelings about you. It's like the new car you buy. Once it's yours, you tend to look past its warts or even find the warts quirky and appealing. Parents who requested you will do the same. You'll get the benefit of the doubt because people hate admitting they were wrong.

Parents who like you, students who like you, parents and students who want you as their teacher, the benefit of the doubt. That sounds like a recipe for lasting happiness to me.

6. See the Big Picture

I once attended a presentation during which the speaker bemoaned how much money professional athletes were paid relative to what teachers earn. The presenter used Michael Jordan's salary and endorsement deals to calculate the number of dollars Jordan earned every *minute* of his life. It was a lot. The teachers ate it up. "America cares more about sports than it does about education," is the prevailing wisdom, especially among educators.

Every year there's a story about an athlete holding out for a bigger deal or a TV show on the verge of cancellation because an actor won't renew his contract without more money. Because these are people who have already made millions of dollars, we incredulously ask: **How much more do they need?**

Well, how much more do *you* need? What amount of money would make *you* happy?

Would $200 million be enough? It wasn't for NBA Hall of Famer Allen Iverson, who made more than that over the course of his career and is now broke.[35] Or how about Marilyn Monroe, with a net worth of $27 million, who married and divorced three times, struggled with her fame, and whose final years were filled with illness, personal problems, a rapidly declining professional reputation, and a probable suicide when she was just 36 years old?

But those are famous people with unique problems, you argue. You're just a regular teacher who, if the lucky beneficiary of a sudden windfall, would know how to handle it.

Then consider Les Robbins, a Wisconsin teacher who won a $111 million Powerball jackpot. Of the win, he says, "It definitely changed my life. Obviously, it changed in both positive **and negative** ways."[36] High school teacher Craig Henshaw won $21 million in 2011 and intended to keep doing the job he loved. But his work environment became toxic as co-workers badgered him to pay off their loans. It got so bad he had to resign. He estimates he lost a quarter of his friends over the win.[37]

We can't buy happiness with more money, in spite of how often we tell ourselves we can.

Perhaps you still don't believe me. Maybe you think that you really *would* be happy if only you were rich. Just because it didn't work out for some of those other fools, you would know how to handle it. You would be happy. Okay. Then think about this:

The average world income is $5,000. If you make more than $5,000 per year, you are in the top *half* of earners in the world. You're better off than 3.5 *billion* people if you make just $416 per month.

According to the National Education Association, the average first-year teacher in the U.S. earns $36,141.[38] If you're a woman — and three-fourths of U.S. teachers are — then that income puts you in the 67th percentile for all female earners in the U.S. You're in the top third! If you're a male first-year teacher earning the average, your income places you in the 48th percentile of all males. Regardless of your gender, the average first-year American teacher makes more money than 57 percent of all U.S. workers. Open the phone book (if you can still find one). Pick two names. Odds are you earn more than one of them.

According to Glassdoor, the average teacher salary in the U.S. is $45,263.[39] That figure puts the average American teacher in the top 0.41 percent of the richest people in the world. That's right, teachers are one-percenters. Actually, we're one-half of one-percenters. In other words, if you want to be rich, you can stop because you already are!

(To find out exactly where you and your salary rank, enter your figures at www.globalrichlist.com.)

But you object. I'm comparing American teachers to every job in the entire world! It's ridiculous to compare teachers to kids working in a sweatshop in some third-world country. I should compare teachers to other American, college-educated professionals.

I don't have to. Neil Pasricha does exactly that in his book, *The Happiness Equation*. Here's the table he provides, comparing the hourly rate of pay for a Harvard MBA, a retail assistant manager, and a teacher:

	Harvard MBA	Retail Asst. Mgr.	Teacher
Salary	$120,000	$70,000	$45,000
Vacation	2 weeks	2 weeks	12 weeks
Weeks Working/Year	50 weeks	50 weeks	40 weeks
Hours/Week	85	50	40
Hours/Year	4,250	2,500	1,600
Pay/Hour	$28	$28	$28

Before you slam Pasricha as another ignoramus who hates teachers' unions, you should know that both his dad and wife are teachers. You can read more about how he came up with the above numbers in his book, but when you do this type of comparison, it's obvious that teachers' claims of poverty are mostly hyperbole.

But you already knew that money can't buy happiness. It's not money you want, it's respect. Teachers just aren't respected in America! Doctors, lawyers, actors, and athletes! These are the people Americans admire! Right?

Well, no. From 1977 to 2009, Harris Interactive polling has asked the following question:

I am going to read off a number of different occupations. For each, would you tell me if you feel it is an occupation of very great prestige, considerable prestige, some prestige, or hardly any prestige at all?

In 2009, 73 percent of respondents said teachers had considerable or very great prestige. Only firefighters, scientists, doctors, nurses, and military officers scored higher. That's good company.[40]

70 percent of respondents to a 2013 Gallup poll rated grade school teachers "very high" on honesty and ethical standards. They ranked under only nurses and pharmacists. In a 2011 poll, 62 percent of respondents rated high school teachers "very high" on those same standards, in contrast to just 47 percent for clergy, 54 percent for police officers, and 24 percent for journalists.[41]

Teachers also have more scheduled days off than other professions. Most of our contractual days are just seven hours, 30 minutes of which is designated a duty-free lunch. We also get to work primarily with kids, who are more fun, imaginative, honest, and trusting, and who laugh 20 times more often than adults.

Teachers have already won. We are wealthy beyond most of the world's wildest dreams. Our jobs have perks others would love to have. **So how much more do you need?**

A large part of being happy is realizing how good you have it.

7. Choose Optimism

I can hear your arguments. Some of you are shouting them.

- Other people with similar education levels and experience make more money than I do.

- Inflation outpaces teacher salary increases, so my purchasing power has actually gone down.

- I have to work a second job to pay off my student loans.

- I can't save enough to send my kids to college.

- I don't care what those fancy polls say, my profession is certainly not respected!

- The public may trust me, but my administration sure doesn't, and neither do some of my students' parents.

- I don't have that much time off! While students are resting, I'm checking papers, planning lessons, attending trainings, working a part-time job, teaching summer school, taking classes (at my own expense, thank you very much!), and getting my room cleaned and ready for next year.

- Seven-hour days? On what planet? I get to school early, leave late, and take work home with me almost every day. Even with ten-hour days, I always feel behind.

Okay, I hear you.

I admit to biased reporting in the previous chapter. I admit to biased thinking in the way I view the world. That bias is called optimism. Because here's the truth: If you want to tell yourself that you're underpaid, disrespected, mistrusted, and generally unappreciated by society, you can certainly find evidence to support that view. But if you want to believe that you are rich, respected, trusted, and valued, there's evidence for that, too. Since it's up to you to choose what to believe, why not choose to view the world and your place in it in a way that will make you happy?

Maybe you'd like to view the world more optimistically. Perhaps you've tried in the past, only to revert to negative self-talk, harmful social comparisons, and a damaging pessimistic worldview. Choosing optimism can be harder than it seems.

You can blame your brain. Our brains focus on negative thoughts more than positive ones even though we have three times as many positive experiences than negative. In his book *If You're So Smart, Why Aren't You Happy?*, Raj Raghunathan describes a "mental chatter" exercise he's given to over 1,500 students. The exercise requires participants to record their thoughts for two weeks. Before starting, the students are asked to predict what percentage of their thoughts will be positive. Most predictions fall between 60 and 75 percent. What Raghunathan and others have found is that 50 to 70 percent of our thoughts are actually *negative*.

Your brain has a negativity bias, which means it reacts more strongly to bad stuff than good stuff. Psychologists believe it's an evolutionary defense. Our survival depended on our ability to avoid danger, so the brain developed systems to predict, notice, and respond to perceived threats and negative stimuli. Our ancestors paid more attention to the wolf on the other side of the majestic river than they did to the majesty of the river. We're left with this overprotective revenant today, which explains why negative political ads work better than positive ones, why the news continues to adhere to "if it bleeds, it leads," and why when your principal gives you a two in one area of your evaluation, you obsess over it to the exclusion of the many threes and fours you received in other areas.

Our negativity bias makes optimism challenging. It also pervades the educational experience. We spend a lot of time focusing on our failures and very little time celebrating our successes. We spend far more time and money on remediation efforts for students who struggle than we do on enrichment opportunities for those who thrive. In the classroom, we direct most of our attention to those who are behind and very little to those who are ahead. When we talk about our students with colleagues, we discuss our challenges more than our successes. We complain about the two students who had bad mornings and don't mention, or even think about, the vast majority of students who did well.

When we think about our jobs and our futures, negativity takes hold again. We expect that student behavior will get worse over time, that parents will become less involved, and that we'll have more needy students in the future than we do now. We fret over the new Secretary of Education and the future of public schooling in America. We worry about our pensions, privatization, vouchers, and charter schools. We are really good at finding negative things to obsess over. To be an optimist is to wage a never-ending battle against your natural inclination toward pessimism.

Social psychologists have a name for how people explain the events in their lives. They call it an "explanatory style." A pessimist blames himself for bad news, assumes the current situation will never change, and that a negative event will affect all areas of his life.

An optimist tends to credit herself for good news but blame bad news on circumstances out of her control. She assumes good things will last and bad things won't. She is confident that positive events will spill over into other areas of her life. Optimists engage in cognitive reframing that avoids assuming the worst and instead assumes the best. Let's look at an example of how optimists and pessimists would explain the same event.

You're a few minutes late to lunch, and you rush into the teachers' lounge to grab your food from the refrigerator. As you sit down, you notice that the chatter from the other teachers has died down. They are all getting up and exiting the lounge. You're left to eat alone.

A pessimist would tell herself that her colleagues don't like her. She's done something to offend them. Maybe they've never liked her and aren't even pretending to anymore. It won't matter what she does, because they're never going to like her. Her workplace is going to become a toxic place. She may have to resign.

An optimist would frame the same event in a completely different way. She would tell herself that her colleagues must have had some responsibility that required them to shorten their lunches. Their leaving had nothing to do with her arrival; it was simply a coincidence. Perhaps they were meeting with some students or needed to finish some work before students returned for the afternoon session. Whatever the reason, she will now enjoy a peaceful and pleasantly silent lunch.

Not having any definitive evidence either way, optimists choose to believe the explanation that is more charitable to themselves. Having the same information, pessimists blame themselves, feel helpless to change their circumstances, and assume the worst eventual outcome.

You can practice reframing events whenever you have a negative thought. You can also practice finding the silver lining in what most people perceive as bad news. Almost everything that happens to us can be viewed negatively or positively.

You think your principal has it out for you? He likely doesn't, but even if he does, there's a good chance he won't be around for long. While national data doesn't exist, the average tenure for a high school principal in Texas is just three years.[42] Many teachers work for a high number of principals over the course of their careers. I've had five in seventeen years.

The lowest reader in all of second grade was placed in your class? Lots of room to improve and demonstrate your effectiveness as a reading teacher.

Your classroom has a leak and you're being moved to the library? The change of location will keep things fresh and interesting. Plus, look at all the books the kids can read when they finish their work!

The worst-behaved kid in the school will be on your roster? The principal must think highly of your classroom management and relationship-building skills.

The best reason to be optimistic is that it beats being pessimistic. More than one study has shown that optimistic people have lower blood pressure. A study conducted by Harvard and Boston University scientists found that pessimistic men were more than twice as likely to develop heart disease than optimistic men between ages 61 and 71.[43]

According to studies from the U.S. and the Netherlands, optimism increases longevity. In a 10-year study of about one thousand subjects age 65 to 85, researchers found those with the sunniest dispositions were 45 percent less likely to die than those with the bleakest outlooks.[44]

Since you have a say in the matter, why not choose the mindset that will make you happier, healthier, and allow you to live longer? Become annoyingly good at finding the bright side. Be an incorrigible optimist. You'll be a much happier teacher.

8. Be Grateful

Two women go to the beach. To be old-fashioned, let's call them Alice and Betty. The beach is busy because it's a beautiful summer day. Alice and Betty find an agreeable spot to place their belongings and lay out a blanket. They're close enough to a group of young people that they can overhear large chunks of their conversation.

Alice finds it annoying. She came to the beach for peace and quiet. She tries to block the voices out, but that only makes it worse. There's also a small boy playing in the water by himself. He's farther from the shore than Alice likes, and she can't help worrying about him. What if there's an undertow? The seagulls are intrusive. They strut around the sand, waiting for handouts, which, to her disbelief, some people are actually providing. It's like they want the damn gulls there! The sun is hotter than she likes. There's barely a breeze. She'd go in the water, but it's too cold, and besides, people would look at her. She's not comfortable in her bikini.

Betty enjoys the teenagers' conversation. It triggers memories of her own high school days when she'd come with her friends to this very beach. She eavesdrops and is encouraged that the topics of conversation aren't any different than when she was that age. Maybe she's not that old, she thinks. Betty notices a boy bravely wandering farther from the shore and silently thanks his parents for allowing their kid to take some risks in life. It's nice to see a kid playing without Mom and Dad hovering over-protectively. Betty doesn't mind the gulls. They're funny birds, and she admires their boldness. It's not many birds that will come so close to people. The sun feels great, nice and hot, and there's no breeze to blow sand in her face when people walk past. The water is cold, but it makes for a great contrast. A quick dip is enough to cool her off for a good 20 minutes.

Who's having the better time at the beach, despite the exact same circumstances?

Who is happier?

Who would you rather be, Alice or Betty?

Who are you more often?

It's easy to become preoccupied with small annoyances until they're all we notice. While teaching a lesson, our eyes zero in on Ashley playing with a cootie catcher, and we ignore all of the other students intently looking back at us. After checking papers, we're disheartened over the handful of students who did poorly and feel no pride at all over the students who did well.

It's natural to do this, but that doesn't mean we have to accept it. It's natural to defecate in the woods, but I don't do it unless it's an emergency. So since we're fighting human nature when we choose to be optimistic, we need a way to force it on ourselves until it becomes a habit. Regularly expressing gratitude is one way to do this.

A 2012 survey evaluated American attitudes toward gratitude. It found that while 90 percent of people report being grateful for their family and 87 percent are grateful for their friends, only 52 percent of women and 44 percent of men regularly express their gratitude to others. They were least grateful at work. 74

percent rarely or never expressed gratitude toward their boss.[45]

Expressing gratitude at work is easy to do. Teachers are giving people. Not a day goes by that someone in my building doesn't do something for me. I've had teachers share materials, trade recess duty days, give me food when I forgot my lunch, rearrange schedules to accommodate my needs, hold open doors while my hands were full, bring donuts for the staff, put my copies in my mailbox so they didn't get mixed in with all the others, and any number of other small favors that I appreciate. But like most people, I don't often express my gratitude. A simple verbal thank you would do it. I could also send a short email or text. A couple of years ago I bought a large box of cheap thank you cards that I keep above my desk for when students bring me gifts. I should buy some more for the generous adults I work with.

One way to increase your gratitude is to keep a gratitude journal. There have been many studies on the effects of keeping a gratitude journal on people's happiness. Dr. Robert Emmons of the University of California-Davis worked with three experimental groups over ten weeks. One group recorded five things they were grateful for in the last week. The second group wrote down five hassles. The third group simply listed things that occurred over the previous week. At the end of the ten weeks, the gratitude group felt better about their lives, were more optimistic about their futures, and reported fewer physical complaints. Other studies have shown that people who keep gratitude journals were more likely to make progress toward personal goals and more likely to report having helped others with personal problems.

If you've never tried it and you want to increase your happiness at work, start listing things you're grateful for. Appreciate those things you like about your job that you may take for granted. Here are some ideas to get your started:

- You have a job!
- You make more money than almost everyone on the planet!
- You get to hang out with kids. They keep you young!
- You have your own office — in fact, an entire room. Your room is bigger than many CEOs' offices!
- Your job provides frequent social interaction.
- Your job is mentally stimulating. Every day is different!
- Your job matters. You're a part of something bigger than you. You're not here earning money for some company, but shaping the lives of young people.

The reason expressing gratitude works is because it acts as a counter to habituation. Unfortunately, we tend to take our lives for granted, because after awhile, no matter how good we have it, we become accustomed to things we used to appreciate.

My first paycheck was a little more than $700. I felt like King Midas! After putting pizza on my credit card while student teaching for a year, I had actual money! I could buy 70 pizzas!

Now I have no idea how I survived on such a meager amount. By being grateful for what we have, we recognize all of the blessings of our lives. We become content instead of constantly desiring more under the mistaken belief that acquisitions will lead to greater happiness.

Social psychologist Sonja Lyubomirsky, author of *The How of Happiness* and *The Myths of Happiness*, calls gratitude a "meta-strategy" because it boosts happiness in so many ways. Gratitude helps us focus less on ourselves and connects us to other people. It counters the hubris we sometimes feel about our own accomplishments by acknowledging that we achieved success with the help of others.

Martin Seligman, the "father of positive psychology," recommends an exercise he calls Three Blessings. Every night before you go to sleep, think of three good things that happened. Write them down. Reflect and write about why they happened. The Three Blessings exercise forces you to focus on the good things in your life. So many people go to bed worrying about things or reliving their failures from the day. Three Blessings allows you to express gratitude for all the good things that happened to you. Remember, research tells us that we have three times more positive experiences than negative. If it doesn't feel that way to you, it's because you're thinking more about the negative ones.

Seligman also recommends teaching these strategies to students, which is just what 2003-2004 Michigan Teacher of the Year Bill Cecil does. He calls it "Name Three." In his book, *Best Year Ever,* Cecil writes, "At the start of each morning, ask your students to write down three things they're excited, happy, or proud of. These things don't have to be big in their lives. They can be little things such as excitement or pleasure about the cereal they ate for breakfast that morning."[46]

A second exercise Seligman recommends is a "gratitude visit." In his book *Flourish*, he writes:

"Your task is to write a letter of gratitude to this individual and deliver it in person. The letter should be concrete and about three hundred words: be specific about what she did for you and how it affected your life. Let her know what you are doing now, and mention how you often remember what she did. Make it sing! Once you have written the testimonial, call the person and tell her you'd like to visit her, but be vague about the purpose of the meeting; this exercise is much more fun when it is a surprise. When you meet her, take your time reading your letter."[47]

Other research has proven that simply the act of writing such a letter will boost your happiness, regardless of whether you ever send it or read it aloud.

Teachers love to receive letters or see Facebook posts from former students who express gratitude toward them. Why not do this yourself? Think of a former teacher or colleague who impacted you. Write them a letter. Write a letter to the people in your life who often go unappreciated, like your school custodian, your mail lady, your child's school bus driver, or a day care provider. I have a colleague who takes to Facebook every day during the month of November to express gratitude for all sorts of things in her life. Reading her posts boosts my happiness and makes me more appreciative of the blessings in my own life.

We direct so much of our energies to preparing students for future success in the belief that if they succeed, they will be happy. But success doesn't guarantee happiness. So why not teach students scientifically proven strategies to directly increase their levels of happiness? Just as we try to give them tools that will help them function at work and in society, we should provide them with strategies to enhance their happiness. Someday, they might be grateful that you've done so. They may even write you a letter, call you up, and read it to you.

Regularly expressing gratitude is a way to force yourself to notice the good things around you. It helps you fight against your natural tendency to focus on the negative. It compels you to be more optimistic, which will make you happier. It will make you an Alice and not a Betty.

9. Believe in Something Bigger

Research consistently shows that religious people are happier than nonreligious people. According to a study by the Austin Institute for the Study of Family and Culture, 45 percent of people who attend religious services on a weekly basis describe themselves as "very happy." Of those who never attend church, only 28 percent said the same.[48]

Pew Research found that people who are highly religious are more engaged with their extended families, more likely to volunteer, more involved in their communities, and are generally satisfied with their lives. Nearly half of highly religious Americans got together with extended family at least once or twice a month. Just 30 percent of less-religious Americans did. 65 percent of highly religious adults said they had donated money, time, or goods in the past week, compared with 41 percent who were less religious.[49]

Research by Chaeyoon Lim and Robert Putnam found that when you statistically control for social relationships, the association between religion and happiness disappears.[50] In other words, religious people have more social connections through their congregations, and it is that frequent social interaction that accounts for increased well-being, not religion itself.

Additional research has found the propensity toward charity and volunteerism among the religious to be connected with higher happiness.[51] So while it appears that a belief in God and church attendance lead to happier lives, research suggests that social connectedness, giving, and volunteerism may be the actual causes of higher reported well-being.

Psychologists also surmise that religious people get a boost of happiness from believing in something larger than themselves. Religious people cope with illness better than the nonreligious, perhaps because they can lean on the support network of their fellow parishioners, or because their belief in God allows them to turn the matter over to His capable hands.

A person's specific religion or denomination does not seem to matter as much as the fact that he or she believes in something. Religion, like environmentalism, animal activism, or dedicating your life to helping those in poverty, provides a higher purpose in life and it is this that contributes to a person's well-being.

All of this is great news for teachers. Our jobs place us in the company of others. We have a built-in support network of colleagues who are going through similar struggles. We give our time, money, and energy to our students. Many of us volunteer additional time at after-school events. One of the oft-cited benefits of teaching kids is that we are part of something larger than ourselves. It's a reason teachers rate highly on surveys of well-being. We know that when we get up in the morning our work will have purpose and that its impacts can be felt outside the walls of the school and deep into the future.

Unlike religion, a belief in our far-reaching influence and in the importance of what we do does not require faith. It's evidenced in the stories that former students tell about their teachers.

President Bill Clinton credits his high school band director, Virgil Spurlin, with making him into the person he became. Clinton said, "He was unbelievable. All my life I thought of him.

I stayed in touch with him on and off until he passed away. I really felt that my early years with him convinced me that I could organize and run things. That I could do whatever I wanted to do and that I could actually marshal other people in a common effort, and of course if you're in politics that's very important."[52]

Oprah Winfrey said, "I know I wouldn't be where I am today without my fourth grade teacher, Mrs. Duncan."

Bill Gates attributes some of his success to a number of teachers:

"A lot of the teachers there were very encouraging in my math and science and giving me the books that they liked, letting me read ahead. And the whole computer experience, the exposure came because Lakeside was sort of forward-looking. They were truly amazing — that when the teachers found it too confusing, they let the students take over. Most schools would have just, I don't know, shut the thing down or something. It was a very weird deal where we kind of took charge and even the whole way we started using computers to pick when the classes would meet — that was a friend and I in charge of doing that. So they had a comfort, and you know, there were a few teachers that I would give a lot of credit to — they let us go and dream about where we would take it."[53]

Those who laud their teachers don't recall individual lessons or specific activities. They say they were inspired, given confidence, challenged, trusted, set free to explore, or introduced to something new. The lesson for teachers who want to make a real difference in people's lives is to focus on the individual. Reframe how you think about your job. Go back to why you became a teacher in the first place. Aspire to inspire, not just educate. Decide on a vision for your classroom and career.

I review and rewrite my vision each August as I'm gearing up for another school year. It is my guiding philosophy. It prioritizes my decisions. It is what I am about when I am at work. My number one mission is to be a destination classroom. My goal as a third grade teacher is for every second grader to want to be in my class badly enough that they bother their parents about it.

To accomplish this, I want my classroom to be:

- a place of trust
- positive and friendly
- fun
- organized and well-managed
- a place where hard work is expected and success is celebrated

I also set personal goals for each year. Working toward meaningful goals is a proven way to increase happiness. If your district's strategic plan doesn't speak to you, or if your school's SMART goals don't align with your passions, then set your own targets and measure your success against those. I type mine up before every school year. They are the goals I review and assess, and the only ones I truly care about.

Know who you are. Know what matters most to you. Imbue your work with meaning, and strive to make a difference in the lives of your students. You'll reap the benefits of having a purpose in life. You will be a happier teacher.

10. Give

By our natures, we teachers are giving people. Our students get the best hours of our lives. They get most of our energy. They get our most creative ideas. We deplete our limited stores of patience while in their presence. They get our inspiration and our perspiration. They get our best selves, while our families get whatever is left after our exhausting days.

We give our time. While the contractual day for most teachers is about seven hours, the NEA reports that we spend an average of 50 hours per week on instructional duties, with 12 of those hours being non-compensated activities like checking papers on nights and weekends, bus duty, club advisories, lesson planning, and meeting with parents.[54]

We give our money. Most teachers must pay out of pocket for continuing education credits to maintain their certifications. According to the Education Market Association, the average teacher spends nearly $500 on classroom supplies each year. One in ten spend over $1,000. An entire business, Teachers Pay Teachers, wouldn't exist if teachers didn't willingly shell out large sums of their own dough to improve their instruction.

So you would be justified in asking what more we could, or should, possibly give. Teachers already spend all day serving others. Indeed, combined with the meaning we find in our work, our consistent giving may explain why teachers report such high levels of satisfaction with their lives. Giving more isn't something we should expect from teachers, but teachers who want more happiness should know what the research says.

In one experiment, researchers approached students on a university campus and gave them a $5 or $20 bill to spend by the end of the day. They instructed half the participants to spend the money on themselves, and half to spend the money on someone else. That evening, the participants who had been assigned to spend the money on someone else reported feeling happier over the course of the day than those assigned to spend the money on themselves.[55]

Another study found that in 120 of 136 countries, there was a positive relationship between giving and happiness, and this relationship was significant in a majority of countries.[56]

In a third study, toddlers were given treats, such as Goldfish crackers. A few minutes later, they were asked to give one of the treats away to a puppet, who happily "ate" it. The experimenter then pretended to find a bonus treat and asked the child to give this to the puppet as well. The children's reactions were videotaped and later rated for happiness. When toddlers shared their "own" treat with the puppet, they displayed greater happiness than when they gave away the extra treat provided by the researcher.[57] Psychologists believe that humans possess a penchant for giving and that we are hardwired to benefit from it.

As teachers, we have many opportunities to give to our students, colleagues, and parents. One of the best things we can give our students is excellent teaching. In his book, *The Happy Teacher Habits*, Michael Linsin shares a lesson planning strategy he uses that engages students from the start. It consists of the following three steps:

1. Select a single objective for your lesson. Choose just one thing you want your students to understand or accomplish.

2. Find one noteworthy aspect about your objective that you can "sell" to your students. It can be interesting, surprising, weird, gross, funny, or sad, but it must be something that will cause students to sit up and take notice.

3. Connect the information by telling a story. Storytelling engages. If you've ever told your students a story from your personal life, you know how attentive they get. Use this powerful technique to hook your students and deliver the content you want students to learn.

Here's an example: I teach third grade social studies in Michigan. As part of our Michigan history curriculum, students learn about French settlements in the Great Lakes region. A huge part of this story is the fur trade. So if I'm going to teach about the fur trade, I would start by identifying one objective for the lesson:

1. Objective: Students will understand why the fur trade was a source of conflict in North America.

2. Hook: I say, "Think of something you really really want, but can't have. Something so expensive your parents won't buy it for you. Something so expensive you might

never be able to buy it for yourself." I then display a photograph of a man wearing a beaver pelt hat and build interest by saying, "At one time, the hat on this man's head was like that thing. Very few people could afford to buy a hat like this. That made it valuable. Lots of people wanted it, but only rich people could afford it. The hat on this man's head made some people very wealthy. It also led to the deaths of thousands of people. How can a hat cause the deaths of thousands of people? That's what you're going to learn today."

3. Storytell: "I have a younger brother, and when we were growing up, we shared a bedroom. Sometimes we didn't get along too well, and one time we'd had enough of each other. We begged our parents to let one of us move into the den, but they were having none of it. They told us to solve our own problem. So we decided to split the room in half. At night, we'd sleep in our bunkbed, but any other time we had to stay on our side of the room. We taped a line down the middle of it. We chose sides and thought we'd solved our problem. But it wasn't long before we had more problems. The stereo was on my brother's side, so he could play whatever music he wanted, and I had to listen to it. The door was on my side of the room. We agreed that we could both use the door, but the basketball hoop attached to the top of the door was all mine. So I was the only one who could play basketball. But sometimes the ball would cross the tape, and my brother would keep it just to make me angry. And I did get angry. We would yell at each other and fight. The tape actually caused more problems than it solved."

At this point, I would transition to the idea of borders and how Great Britian and France had claimed different (and sometimes the same) lands. Students could then look at maps and investigate the locations of forts and trading posts. An analogy could be made between the stereo and basketball hoop and the most desirable areas for fur trapping or water routes. Students could then begin to understand why there were conflicts.

If this style of teaching is unfamiliar to you, you might be nervous to try it. Most people ask themselves if they *can* do something before they try. They then ask if they *want* to do that thing. Only then, after they have decided that they *can* do it and that they *want* to do it, will they try something new.

I've done this with roller skating. I never roller skated as a child, so when my daughter wanted to learn, I told her I couldn't teach her. I knew I couldn't do it because I never had before. I knew I didn't want to do it because I didn't want to look like an idiot or break any important bones. Therefore, I didn't do it.

Kids don't think like this. They try first. Visit an elementary school playground sometime and watch how the youngest among them grab onto the monkey bars with an unsettling lack of fear. I have recess duty twice a week. During the first few weeks of each school year, I regularly rescue a number of kids. That doesn't stop them from trying again. Kids see someone do something and they want to do it, too. Once they try it, they believe they can do it. Once they believe they can do it, they become motivated to keep trying. They try, realize that failure isn't that big of a deal, and then try again. They get a little bit better, which motivates them to try some more. Eventually, they do it! It's why many kids learn to ride their bikes not from their well-meaning and patient parents, but from being around other kids who are already riding.

Take this growth mindset into your teaching. If you've never started a lesson with storytelling, try it. Once you do, you'll realize it's probably better than the way you have been starting lessons. Then you'll decide that 1. You can do it, 2. It's kind of fun, and 3. You'll wonder if you can get better at it, which will lead you to try some more. Try enough times, and it will become easier as you become more skilled. Serve your students engaging lessons. It's one of the best things you can give them.

But don't stop there. Other ways to boost your happiness at work through giving include:

- Giving advice to other teachers
- Giving away teaching materials you no longer use
- Donating books to families or a new teacher who doesn't have much of a classroom library
- Contributing money to an employee scholarship for students
- Buying a colleague's lunch
- Contributing to a staff member's baby or wedding shower gift
- Donating canned goods to needy families
- Buying toys for needy families for Christmas
- Purchasing a backpack and filling it with back-to-school supplies
- Paying off the lunch account balances of needy students
- Finding a worthy project on Donors Choose to give to
- Giving money to a Go Fund Me project to help a school family going through a challenging time

Earlier in this chapter, you read about the college students who were happier when they gave away money instead of spending it on themselves. The most interesting part of that study is that the researchers asked other participants to predict which act would make them happier. They believed that they would be happier spending it on themselves.

Remember, we aren't very good at predicting our future feelings. Giving is a perfect example. Studies show that people believe they will feel pain from giving, but they actually feel proud. Don't believe the science? Do it right now. Hop onto Donors Choose or Go Fund Me and find a project that speaks to you. Give. I guarantee you won't regret it. In fact, you'll probably feel better about yourself. You'll feel happier.

11. Stop Worrying

I was at a science training a few months ago when I received a text message from my principal.

Principal: I have a feeling your students are on games they should not be on.

Me: Most of them play games during short breaks I give them between subjects. Which games?

Principal: Some zombie game.

At this point, I decided to stop texting. I spent the next 30 minutes worrying. Was I in trouble for the sites my students were visiting on their Chromebooks? How much trouble was I in? What would the principal do?

Then I got angry. How did the principal become involved with this anyway? Is there some guy sitting in the technology office with nothing better to do than spy on my students' Internet activity?

Then I got defensive. What's the difference between giving students five minutes to play a mindless game and taking a five-minute "brain break" to play Simon Says? The district spent all this money on Chromebooks. Can we not use them for non-academic fun every once in awhile?

I was worked up by the time I realized that my imagination had likely run away with itself and I should just call my principal to find out what was up. As it turned out, he'd walked through the room to see how my substitute was doing, and the sub told him about the games because he was unsure if students were supposed to be on them. My principal had texted me for clarification. We agreed that for today, since I wasn't there, the kids would stay off the game site. No big deal. I'd spent 30 minutes worrying for no reason, which is usually the case when we worry.

All worries start with the same question: "What if?"

- What if I get fired?
- What if I'm late for the meeting?
- What if that angry parent emails my principal?
- What if I get a flat tire out here in the middle of nowhere?
- What if she says no when I ask her out?
- What if my kid gets kidnapped?

All worry is fear of what *could* happen.

But lots of things *could* happen. Aliens could invade and enslave all of us, but most of us don't spend much time worrying about it because we consider the possibility remote and therefore not worth worrying about.

As silly as that example is, there's a lesson in it. Much of what we worry about is unlikely, some of it *very* unlikely, and yet we worry anyway. We allow fear to stress us out. We can't predict the future. We certainly can't control it. That makes worrying about it pointless. The next time you worry, ask yourself two questions:

1. **Is there a problem in the external world?**
2. **Is there something I can do about it right now?**

If the answer to those two questions is yes, then exercise control over the situation. The mere act of doing something will often ease your concern. In my example at the start of this chapter, my worrying stopped when I called my principal. Within seconds, I realized I had no reason to be worried. The antidote to worry is action.

I once had a principal who, when she wanted to meet with me, would say, "Paul, can we schedule a time to talk?" But she wouldn't tell me what she wanted to talk about. Being a normal human with a normal human mind, I always assumed the worst. I'd spend the whole day worrying about it. Inevitably, it would be something unimportant that I needn't have worried about at all. It would have been far more productive of me to simply ask my principal what she wanted to discuss. When you can exercise control over a situation to relieve your concerns, do so.

People have a fundamental need to feel in control. We love the feeling of control so much that most of us would rather drive than fly,[58] even though we're far more likely to die in a car accident than a plane crash.

One thing we can't always control is our thoughts, and it drives us crazy. Fears arrive unbidden, demanding our attention and triggering our body's stress response. Our hearts speed up, our palms sweat, we become distracted. Our breathing changes. Worrying taxes our bodies, and we react to it the same way we react to danger.

But worry is not danger, it's doubt.

We don't know what will happen, and that bothers us because we tend to assume the most horrific outcomes our dark imaginations can conjure. That fear feels threatening. We may not be able to control all our thoughts, but that doesn't mean we have to allow them to control us.

Everybody worries. People differ in how they respond to worry.

It is the relationship with worry that makes the difference between people who seem to never have a care in the world and those wracked with anxiety. Those who struggle the most with worry treat it as danger instead of doubt. As a result, they treat the symptom with the wrong medicine. That's bound to backfire, and when it does, it can cause even more worry.

If there is no problem in the external world, then there's nothing to worry about in the first place. If there's nothing you can do about the problem right now, then there's also no reason to worry. In that case, worrying won't change the helplessness of your situation. It's like that old Erma Bombeck quote: "Worry is like a rocking chair: it gives you something to do but never gets you anywhere."

Sometimes my daughter will leave the house to go play with one of her friends in the neighborhood. They're gone for a couple of hours. My wife starts getting concerned after about 30 minutes. What if she gets hit by a car? What if she gets kidnapped? I don't worry because I answer the two questions:

1. Is there a problem in the external world?

No. Therefore, there is nothing to worry about.

2. Is there anything I can do about it right now?

Since there isn't a problem, there isn't anything to do. But if a problem were to arise, I would then reassess. For instance, if she came home with a bloody head, there would be a problem, but there would also be things I could do about it, like wrap her head in gauze and tell her to stop running into hard objects.

The reality is that most of what we worry about will never happen. It helps to remind ourselves of that. Reconsider the fears earlier in this chapter.

What if I get fired?

Well, you probably won't. After all, how many teachers do you know that have been fired? But even if it were to happen, you'll likely have a heads-up that the axe is coming. That will give you time to take action, like polish your résumé and look for another job. Maybe even a better one.

What if my daughter gets kidnapped?

75 percent of kidnappings are done by family or friends. The chance that your child will be kidnapped by a stranger is estimated at one in 300,000. The odds of you choking to death are one in 3,400. If you worry about your child getting nabbed whenever they're not under your vigilant supervision, do you also worry about choking to death every time you eat? You should. It's about 100 times more likely to happen.

What if I get a flat tire out here in the middle of nowhere?

When was the last time you got a flat tire? How many times in your life have you gotten a sudden flat while driving? How likely is it to happen right now? Not very? Then stop worrying about it. You might as well worry about the invading aliens and your subsequent enslavement.

What if she says no when I ask her out?

She probably will, so don't ask her out. (Hey, there are times when worrying is a good thing, like when it prevents you from making a total fool of yourself.)

If the unlikely does happen — if you do get that flat 50 miles north of Winnemucca, Nevada — then take action and do something to solve your problem. Try your cell phone. If it doesn't work, wave down another driver and ask for help. Take action, and you'll be too busy solving the problem to worry about it.

Instead of treating worry like danger, treat it for what it is: doubt. Do the opposite of what you normally do when you worry. Instead of fighting or fleeing from the danger, recognize that doubt is simply a form of discomfort. When we feel discomfort, we act to alleviate it or we try to relax and let it pass. The next time you're worried, try this:

1. Acknowledge your doubt, but recognize that it is not danger. Think: "Huh, I guess I don't know what will happen."

2. Determine whether there is anything you can do to influence the outcome or if it's out of your control. If you can do something, do it.

3. Choose fatalism and optimism in your self-talk: "It'll work out whatever way it happens; it usually does. Whatever will be will be. I'll cross that bridge when I get there. God has a plan. Well, things could be worse."

4. Remind yourself that most of your worries never happen. Let facts be your ally. If you're afraid of flying, don't watch *Lost*. Instead, look up the statistical likelihood that you will die in an airplane crash. (I'll save you the trouble. It's one in 11 million. A car accident is one in 5,000. So if you really want to worry, grab that steering wheel with white knuckles and hold on for dear life!)

One of my favorite research findings about worry is reported in the book *If You're So Smart, Why Aren't You Happy?*, by Raj Raghunathan. Raghunathan subjects his college students to something he calls the "Reminisce and Reflect Exercise." He asks them to recall an intensely negative event from two or more years prior. He then asks them to rank how negative the event was at the time and how negative it is now. Finally, he asks them to rank how "meaningful" they now consider the event to be.

It won't surprise you to learn that his students' perceptions of past events change over time. We tend to look at our past through the lens of our present. What is surprising is that the change is more pronounced for negative events than positive ones. Negative events lose their sting faster than positive ones lose their luster. Recalling your first kiss will likely provide you with positive feelings, even many years later, while remembering that time you lost $1,000 at the casino will likely not cause you to feel nearly as terrible as you did at the time (or, more realistically, the next morning).

Raghunathan's favorite finding, however, is that past negative events are much more *meaningful* than past positive events. In fact, the more negative the event, the more meaningful it eventually becomes. That bears repeating in larger letters:

The more negative the event, the more meaningful it eventually becomes.

This is great news for worriers because it means that even if the very thing you fear so much actually happens, you will, at some point in the future, likely cherish its memory. As Sonja Lyubomirsky says in her book, *The Myths of Happiness*, "When we consider the single best thing that happened to us during past years, and the single worst thing, we may be surprised to learn that they are often one and the same."[59]

Negative events teach us lessons we can't learn from positive ones. In time, we come to appreciate those things learned at the school of hard knocks. Negative events also make for great stories that we relish telling once the pain of the event has receded. That lost $1,000 at the blackjack table hurt at the time, but man do people enjoy hearing that story now!

Negative events also lead to opportunities we would not have pursued without them. I used to work with a very unhappy teacher, but he would have continued teaching because it was safe, the pay was good, and he didn't want to go through a career change at his age. When he was asked to resign, I am sure it was a traumatic event. But he soon found a new job he loved in a different field. He made less money, but he was much happier. His new job was less stressful, so he had more energy. He started running every night. He lost weight, smiled more, and felt better about himself. He soon met someone. Two years after he was fired, he was a changed man. He loved his job. He married the girl. They built a house together. He's a completely different person, and none of it would have happened if he hadn't been forced out of his teaching job.

So when it comes to the things you worry most about, remember: They probably won't happen, but even if they do:

- They won't be as bad as you think.

- The pain won't last as long as you think.

- You will likely look back on them positively in the future.

Considering all that, what reason do you still have to worry?

12. Stop Comparing

I'm a third grade teacher, and every year we celebrate a few accomplishments with parties. Whenever my class hits 20 days of perfect attendance, I buy them pizza. For mastering their multiplication facts, we have ice cream sundaes. Occasionally, just because I'm a nice guy, I buy the class donuts.

Also, I like donuts.

Anytime I buy food for the class, I better get the math right. With 28 students, I calculate that I need to buy four pizzas of eight slices each and that I'll eat one slice myself and give away the last three slices to students whose names I draw.

Ice cream is trickier. I usually buy two of those huge tubs but then have to eyeball it as I dish out scoopfuls into waiting bowls, careful to not run out before I serve the last kid.

Even when we do a math activity with Skittles or M&Ms, it's important that every student gets roughly an equal amount.

There will be hell to pay if certain students figure out that their neighbors got a bigger slice, a larger helping of ice cream, or more candy than they did. Even though what these students have is more than they had just minutes before and the result of my charity, they will let me know, in no uncertain terms, the gross injustice of their situation.

This is social comparison at work, and if you think only kids engage in it, you're lying to yourself.

We automatically compare ourselves to others to see how we measure up. We can't stop ourselves from doing it. From childhood, we are sent an unrelenting message that it is better to be better than others. Our parents, teachers, mentors, employers, colleagues, friends, and the media condition us to believe that we should strive to be the best at whatever we do. There are no marketing campaigns telling you to shoot for average. Nobody aims for the fat part of the bell curve.

We chase superiority for many reasons. Part of it is evolutionary: the strongest survive. A second reason is mastery. Humans have a strong need to make progress in pursuit of their most cherished goals. To measure progress, we compare our performance to that of others. We seek superiority to prove to ourselves that we are gaining competence. Superiority also provides us with more freedom. Research shows that people with higher status restrict their words and actions less than people of lower status. A feeling of superiority also enhances our self-worth. Perceiving ourselves as better than others improves our happiness. Many studies have shown that higher-status people enjoy better health outcomes and higher levels of happiness than lower-status people.

Given all that, it may seem that one way to increase your happiness is to chase superiority. But there's a catch. While feeling superior does increase people's happiness, *striving for superiority* has the opposite effect. So although you will improve your health and happiness by being "successful," you will be unhappy for much of the time it took you to achieve that success.

The problem is that in order to feel superior, we have to be able to measure ourselves against other people. The tools we have for performing this measurement aren't very good. Who's the best guitarist of all time, Jimi Hendrix, Jeff Beck, Eddie Van Halen, Eric Clapton, Prince, or somebody else? Who's the best businessman ever? Who's the greatest basketball player to ever grace the hardwood? Who is the world's best teacher?

People don't agree on the answers to the above questions because we don't have very good methods of measuring superiority. If you're striving to become the best teacher, even in your own building, how do you determine your progress toward that goal? Probably the same way everyone else does, by using proxy measurement tools. Since we can't figure out if we're better than others at something, we're forced to look at other metrics, such as wealth, fame, power, influence, number of Twitter followers, end-of-year evaluations, or the number of parent requests we get each year.

One problem with using proxy measures is that they can also be used to measure people's superiority across domains. If I want to determine my place on the social pecking order, I might compare my paycheck to those in other professions. Indeed, many teachers do this. They get upset because people of similar education levels and experience make more than they do. I might compare the size of my house to my neighbor's, even though we have completely different housing needs. I might look around and notice how many people are driving new cars, and then, considering my own clunker, determine that I am falling short in the superiority game.

In other words, because we chase superiority, and because measuring our relative levels of competence is hard to do, we tend to determine our place in the social hierarchy by using measures that are easy to see, such as big houses, expensive clothes, tickets to high-priced events, and other visible and materialistic goods. And there's the rub. Feeling superior feels good.

But striving for superiority does not, because the way we measure our success is almost always by comparing material possessions, and materialism absolutely destroys happiness.

Materialism is an effect of social comparison, which is an effect of our desire to feel superior.

Desire to be superior —> Proof of superiority —> Materialism

People don't buy mansions because they need more space. They don't buy expensive watches because they keep time better. They don't drive a Lexus because it gets them places faster. People purchase luxury items because it makes them feel superior to others. They do so because they think it will make them happier. They're wrong.

When we compare our material goods to others', we are almost always left with feelings of inadequacy and discontent. We might feel jealous or even wronged. What's so special about her? Why aren't my talents recognized? How come he gets paid so much?

The reason materialism fails us is because there will always be someone who is more popular, richer, more attractive, drives a nicer car, and has a better looking spouse. There will also be lots of people who don't have as much as we do, but because of our tendency to pay more attention to negative stimuli, we usually focus on how we come up short. That's a recipe for feelings of inferiority and a blow to our egos and our happiness.

Sonja Lyubomirsky, in her book *The Myths of Happiness*, writes that she studied what could be done about the comparisons we make, since we can't stop ourselves from making them. During her third year of graduate school, she carried out a series of experiments that led her to conclude that, "the secret to being satisfied with our achievements lies not in ignoring other people's strengths and accomplishments, but in not suffering the negative consequences of those observations. In other words, don't let the social comparisons get to you."[60]

Research on self-esteem levels as we age seems to confirm the wisdom of her conclusion. Self-esteem is at its lowest during our teenage years.[61] This is a time when most people are preoccupied with comparing themselves to their peers. In our teenage years, we are actively establishing our places in social pecking orders and constantly assessing how we're stacking up. We compare our friends, our clothing, our attractiveness, our social media followers, our cars, our grades, and gobs of other proxy measures for superiority to those around us.

There are other periods of our lives when we either compare much less or just don't care as much about what we notice. In college, most students, regardless of their parents' wealth, feel relatively poor. In our thirties, most of us are just starting out or we've changed careers. We're still finding our way, and many of our peers have yet to separate themselves from us. Sure, there are a few outliers you read about — those who started a tech company that made them billionaires by age 35 — but most of the people we know are in a similar boat as us — fairly low status, still owing on student loans, leasing an average car, and living in a modest home or apartment.

By our forties, another low period for self-esteem, the separation between ourselves and our cohorts is harder to ignore. Our old college roommate, with whom we once drank Keystone Light because we couldn't afford anything better, is now working in a downtown high-rise, driving a Ferrari, and pretending he never drank Keystone Light. Our friend from high school moved to Colorado, started her own business, participates in triathlons, and just married a CEO who you think you saw on the cover of *Forbes*. That guy who lived down the hall in our college dorm and who was struggling through classes just like us is now a successful accountant, whereas we've been teaching for 15 years and make a modest income but can't afford the big house, nice cars, and exotic vacations others our age regularly share on Facebook.

Speaking of Facebook, a 2016 meta-analysis from Lancaster University found that users were at a greater risk of depression when they made social comparisons, posted frequent negative status updates, accepted former lovers as Facebook friends, and felt jealousy while reading others' posts.[62] Research shows that we tend to believe others on Facebook are better off than we are,[63] and a 2016 study published in the journal Cyberpsychology, Behavior and Social Networking Journal found that taking a break from Facebook led to increased life satisfaction and more positive emotions.[64]

A study from 2011 found that Americans are most happy between the ages of 75 and 79.[65] Perhaps that's because older people have stopped comparing themselves to others and are content with the lives they've lived. Or maybe they do compare, but since a fair number of their peers are now in the ground or struggling with health problems, they find the comparison favorable.

So how do you not let social comparisons get you down? You might be tempted to engage in what social psychologists call "downward comparisons" instead of "upward comparisons." Instead of comparing yourself to those who have more than you, you compare yourself to those who have less. But Lyubomirsky concludes, "When we ask ourselves the question, 'How good am I?' those of us who rely on our own internal objective standards are happiest. The goal, then, is to rely less on others when determining your self-worth and more on your own standards."

Don't ask, "How good am I compared to the teacher across the hall?" Instead ask, "Does my career meet my needs?" or "Am I a better teacher now than I was last year?"

One way teachers can avoid comparing themselves to other teachers is by intentionally not learning about other teachers' evaluations. No matter what you learn, it is likely that at least one other teacher scored higher than you did. Even if you outperformed all but one other teacher in your school or district, you will focus on the fact that you weren't the best. Research has shown that this knowledge will harm your happiness.

You should also ignore government and district labels. Governments love to judge schools, but they use terrible tools and don't know what they're doing anyway. Most legislators have no background in education except as students. Most of their legislation isn't about improving education, but about satisfying some special interest group whose motives are suspect at best.

Ignore website rankings of your school. They've never visited your building, much less your classroom. Dismiss your principal's opinion of you as just one opinion based on a very small sampling of your teaching. Schools need leaders. Principals can have a positive effect on students. But they cannot impact your students like you can. Listen to what they have to say. They're trying their best. They mean well. They want you to succeed. But do not judge yourself based on some numbers derived from one or two 45-minute visits to your classroom out of the more than 1,000 hours you spend teaching each year.

Set standards for your own performance instead. Make them high. Strive to improve your craft. Work hard. Then judge yourself against your own high expectations and ignore all other judgments. Other people's opinions of you are none of your business. As Eleanor Roosevelt famously said, "No one can make you feel inferior without your consent."

As a young teacher, I would read books by Harry Wong, Rafe Esquith, and Ron Clark. They were inspiring, but they also made me feel like a terrible teacher. When I compared my practice to what they wrote about theirs, I felt inadequate. But this is like a college basketball player comparing himself to Lebron James. There is only one Lebron James. There are a handful of other players at a similar level. Everyone else in the world, including other professionals, are way behind Lebron James.

The same is true of teachers. There are teachers out there who are better than you. There always will be. Are you going to let that ruin your happiness? Instead of comparing yourself to others, compare your present self to your past self. Have you improved? Are you a better teacher today than you were last year? What goals do you have for getting better next year?

Many teachers lament their relatively low pay compared to other American professionals. This is a social comparison, and it's no wonder it depresses teachers. The research suggests that a more helpful approach for your well-being is to ask yourself whether your pay satisfies your needs. Do you make enough to live the life you want? Sure, we could all find things to spend extra money on, but if you have secure housing, enough food, a car, and enough to pay for a few luxuries like a Netflix subscription, new shoes, and an occasional vacation, then you may find you're "richer" than you think. What other people earn shouldn't be a concern of yours. Their income has no bearing on your quality of life. Whether or not you earn enough to live a fulfilling life is the standard you should judge your income against.

Remember, just because the metaphorical kid sitting next to you has a bigger slice of metaphorical pizza than you do, you still have pizza. And pizza is really good, even when it's a metaphor.

13. Take Control

Humans are thought to have three basic psychological needs: autonomy, competence, and relatedness.[66] Research across cultures has shown that satisfying these needs is critical for healthy development, engagement, motivation, and well-being. When these needs are not met, people suffer. Since these findings have been documented across many cultures and contexts, scientists believe that the needs are evolutionary rather than learned.

People do not just like having control; we biologically require it. Research suggests that if we lose our sense of control at any point in our lives, we become unhappy, hopeless, and depressed. We need control so badly we are willing to accept the illusion of it in place of the real thing.[67] Even though our rational minds tell us there are situations we cannot control, we don't seem to accept them. People believe they are less likely to get into a car accident if they are driving than if they're riding in the passenger seat. Gamblers throw dice harder when they need higher numbers and softer when they need lower numbers. A survey of 505 people found that 96 percent of them want self-driving vehicles to have steering wheels and pedals, indicating their overwhelming reluctance to give total control over to the car.[68]

Teachers are no different in their need for control. Indeed, many entered the profession because they felt the job would provide more autonomy than other occupations. Research finds that teacher autonomy is positively associated with job satisfaction and retention.[69]

Teachers who believe they have less autonomy are more likely to leave their positions, either by changing schools or quitting altogether.

Regrettably, teachers today feel like they have less control than they did in the past. According to data from the National Center for Education Statistics, educators reported less classroom autonomy in school year 2011-12 than in 2003-04.[70] Studies from the University of Pittsburgh and University of Tennessee identified two key factors – relatively low pay and lack of control and autonomy – that drive teachers away from the profession, with younger and more highly qualified teachers changing careers in greater numbers.

Richard Ingersoll is a former teacher who is now the Board of Overseers Professor of Education and Sociology at the University of Pennsylvania. He's a highly respected researcher who has published over 100 articles on education topics. On teacher attrition, he says:

"The data consistently show us that a big issue is how much voice, how much say, do teachers have collectively in the school-wide decisions that affect their jobs? Teachers are micromanaged. We have been saying for a long time that one size doesn't fit all, all students are different. But teachers are told to stick to the scripted curriculum, which might work for a weaker teacher but it drives good teachers nuts."[71]

"One of the big reasons I quit [teaching] was sort of intangible," Ingersoll says. "But it's very real: It's just a lack of respect. Teachers in schools do not call the shots. They have very little say. They're told what to do; it's a very disempowered line of work."[72]

Teacher autonomy is not just about educators wanting more control. It's a question of trust and professionalism. Governments, school boards, and administrators who trust teachers seek their input in high-stakes decisions and recognize them as the professionals they are by allowing them to decide how to instruct their students. What teachers want is to be trusted.

Louisiana teacher Alice Trosclair, in an article for the *Washington Post*, puts it well:

Trust, pure and simple. Trust that we want the best for our students and society. Trust that 95 percent of us are here for our students and want the best for them, so in turn we give them our best every day.[73]

It's no surprise that teachers feel frustrated. With greater emphasis on standardized test scores came greater accountability for school districts. They reacted by wresting control from teachers. Not trusting teachers to do what was necessary to improve test scores, school districts cut recess time and special classes that weren't directly related to the subjects over which students would be tested. They adopted cookie-cutter programs that they insisted teachers use with fidelity. They enforced pacing guides that required teachers to teach lessons on certain days, regardless of whether students were prepared for them. They mandated test prep sessions. They controlled the selection of curriculum materials, often with limited input from the very people who would be using them. They increased the number of meetings and professional development sessions teachers were required to attend. They forced teachers to collect more data and use that data to justify their decisions. They required more paperwork to remain in compliance with onerous new legislation. And in response to what amounted to a federal bribery scheme, states adopted new teacher evaluation systems that are often arbitrary, capricious, and inconsistent.

The ideal solution would be for society to recognize the wisdom in trusting its teachers with greater control over students' educational experiences. Citizens would then pressure their government and local school boards to allow teachers more input and control over educational decisions. Administrators would operate under the assumption that teachers were doing what was best for students. Everyone would actually trust that teachers were there for their students.

Since that's not likely to happen anytime soon, you shouldn't wait around. You need to exert more control, regardless of how much authorities try to yank it from your grasp. To not do so will lead to frustration, misery, and eventual burnout.

Most teachers still have areas of their day that they can control. Exert it wherever you can. You likely choose your classroom procedures. Most teachers still create their own classroom rules. While many teachers are constricted in some ways with respect to discipline, there is usually still some discretion given to teachers. The standards are mandated, programs your district has approved are also likely required, but how you deliver the content may offer you the chance to control large parts of your day. Most teachers have some choice in how they assess students.

Read your contract to see what you're actually required to do. Many teachers assume they have to do things they don't. I know a former teacher who quit checking homework a few years before he retired. When asked why, he said, "There's nothing in my contract that says I have to check papers."

Perhaps the best way to take control is to start saying no. Many teachers don't like to do this. They want to give as much as they can to their students, and they suspect they'll feel guilty if they don't participate in as many extra activities as their colleagues.

But if you want to be happier at work and you want a long, fulfilling career that allows you to help the greatest number of students, then saying no is a must. School districts regularly take advantage of teachers' giving natures. They ask that we attend after-school events, accommodate parents by holding meetings after hours, and they never provide teachers with enough time to actually do every aspect of their jobs during the workday. It's simply expected that teachers will take work home after school and on weekends.

Successful people say no. In his book, *Essentialism*, Greg McKeown gives the following advice when deciding whether or not to do something: "If it isn't a clear yes, then it's a clear no."

Tim Ferriss, author of *Tools of Titans*, says, "If it's not a 'hell, yeah,' it's a no."

Peter Drucker, the father of modern management thinking and the author of more than three dozen books, believed that "people are effective because they say no."

You cannot do it all. The demands on teachers today are unrealistic. You will burn yourself out trying to meet them all. That means you have to decide what's most important. What's most important for me is my students' learning. If at all possible, I avoid doing anything work-related that doesn't help my students learn. Like every teacher, I have to attend meetings that do nothing to make me more effective in the classroom. But there are other opportunities — committee positions, after-school events, conference opportunities, running a club for students not in my class — that I say no to.

Saying no takes courage. It feels bad. It can temporarily harm the relationship you have with the person making the offer. You might feel guilty when others say yes. Most teachers don't want to rock the boat. We aren't comfortable with disappointing people. But once you learn to say no, you'll find that most of your fears were exaggerated and people will start to respect you more. Since most people don't say no, those who do might not be as well-liked, but they are more admired for their conviction.

The reason you say no is not because you're lazy, but because when you say no to something, you're giving yourself the opportunity to say yes to those things you've prioritized. There is only so much time. Anytime you say yes to something, you are saying no to something else. Determine what it is you want to excel at. Say yes to opportunities that help you reach that goal. Say no to those that don't. When you take charge of your time and zero in on the most essential aspect of your work, you'll be more effective and ultimately more satisfied.

If you're unhappy at work, do something different.

Make changes. The simple choice to act can boost your satisfaction at work because you're exerting control over your situation. Fortunately, the changes you make don't have to be big ones. David Schkade, PhD, a psychologist and professor of management at the University of California San Diego, says that if you transfer even one hour of your day from an activity you hate (commuting, scrubbing the bathroom) to one you like (reading, spending time with friends), you should see a significant improvement in your overall happiness.[74] Taking action is the key. If you hate checking papers after work, stop doing it. If that makes you feel guilty, stop assigning so much homework. If you're required to assign it, assign far less of it or assign long-term projects instead of daily or weekly work. Use the time you previously set aside for checking papers to do something you enjoy, like eating donuts or drinking Keystone Light.

A recent study at the University of Missouri compared college students who made intentional changes, like joining a club or improving their study habits, with others who passively experienced positive turns in their circumstances, such as receiving a scholarship or being relieved of a bad roommate.[75] All the students were happier in the short term, but only the group who made *deliberate* changes stayed that way. Taking control of your life is empowering.

I never used to have a written budget. Some months, I'd spend more than I made. I had no plan for building wealth. I was just sort of hoping to amble my way toward it or hit the Powerball (even though I rarely played). When I finally analyzed my finances, I realized I was spending way too much money eating out. I wrote out a budget and decided where every dollar would go for the month. I earmarked a good chunk of money for college savings for my daughter, my own retirement, and cash savings. Once I had a written plan, I stuck to it. My savings increased much quicker than they ever would have without a budget. I had to plan to build wealth.

It's no different with happiness. You're taking the first step by reading this book. Now start planning how to put these ideas into practice. Don't just hope to stumble onto happiness; plan for it.

14. Strive

It's important for your happiness that you feel successful at work. It's hard to be happy if you're spending a third of your life doing something you suspect you're no good at.

As you've already read, success should be measured against your own standards and not determined through comparisons to others. If you spend too much time doing that, you're bound to determine that you're just not very good, because there's always someone who's going to be better than you (and even if they're not, your negative mind will convince you that they are).

You might define success as having a well-managed classroom with few disruptions to learning. You might measure success by the improvement of your students' writing skills. Success could be assessed through student growth on measurable reading skills or by more subjective means, such as how often students tell you you're their favorite teacher.

In order to achieve frequent feelings of success, teachers need goals. Research shows that goals should be:

- realistic
- flexible
- valued by the culture
- authentic
- not materialistic
- unintrusive on other areas of our lives that lead to happiness.

The more times we achieve our goals, the more competent we feel. A feeling of competence in what we do is an important component of our overall happiness. But teachers should be aware that it isn't the achievement itself that causes lasting happiness. Rather, it is the striving toward mastery that makes us happy. It may be cheesy and something you'd see printed on a bumper sticker, but happiness actually is found in the journey and not the destination.

This is counterintuitive for most of us. We tell ourselves that the reason we work so hard to accomplish our goals is because of the gratification we'll feel when we finally achieve them. And yet once we've reached that destination, we often find that the happiness we expected to feel isn't as intense or as long-lasting as we thought it would be.

My goal when I wrote my first book, *The Teacher's Guide to Weight Loss*, was to finish the book and make it available on Amazon. I wrote a lot some days and a little on others. Every day I wrote I felt good. I was making progress toward my goal. But once I finished the book and started selling it, I wasn't satisfied. I did not sit back and bask in the warm glow of accomplishment. Instead, I changed my goal. Now that the book was done and for sale, I wanted to sell 100 copies of it. Then I wanted 10 good reviews. Then I wanted to make back the money I invested in the enterprise. I kept changing the goal!

After completing the final installment of the Harry Potter series, J.K. Rowling said, "Actually finishing it was the most remarkable feeling I've ever had... [I felt] euphoria, devastated... I was in a hotel room on my own, sobbing my heart out. I downed half a bottle of champagne from the minibar in one and went home with mascara all over my face. It was really tough."[76]

There's no question she was emotional about her massive achievement, but she was also sad that the journey was over. Reading the novels, one can sense how much fun she was having while she wrote them.

When tennis player Pat Cash won Wimbledon, he said, "I had always dreamed of winning and when it happened it was very stressful. It was more of a relief."

Winston Churchill said that success is "stumbling from failure to failure with no loss of enthusiasm." I don't think Churchill meant you had to be a masochist to achieve. Rather, when you are enjoying the journey, failure isn't so bad. Because the process provides you with joy, you don't mind waiting for the payoff.

Accomplishments don't lead to lasting happiness because we move the goalposts, place higher expectations on ourselves, have higher expectations placed upon us by others, and sometimes feel let down because our feelings don't match what we expected to feel when we reached the promised land.

So if reaching a goal doesn't lead to lasting happiness, why should people strive toward goals at all? Because stretching, reaching, working, and making progress *does* make us happy. Researchers Teresa Amabile and Steven Kramer discovered something they call the *progress principle*. Through an analysis of 12,000 workers' diary entries, they found that of all the things that influence happiness at work, the most important was making progress on meaningful goals. Progress occurred on 76 percent of people's best-mood days and setbacks occurred on only 13 percent of those days.[77]

As you take steps toward your goals, you experience dopamine activity in your left prefrontal cortex. Dopamine is a neurotransmitter that helps control the brain's reward and pleasure centers. Once you have achieved what it is you were striving for, you experience what Richard Davidson, a psychology professor at the University of Wisconsin, calls "post-goal attainment positive effect."[78] But this is a short-lived feeling, as the dopamine activity in your brain begins to settle down after the goal has been reached. Because our brains receive an immediate shot of happiness in the form of dopamine following a success, it's better for our longer-term happiness to experience many small successes, otherwise known as progress, than it is to experience infrequent massive successes.

I have the goal of finishing this book. I look forward to the day it's done. But I'm also enjoying the process of writing it. It enhances my happiness because the research has taught me a lot of interesting things. The writing of it has provided additional structure to my days. I've acquired new skills, such as setting up a website, designing 3D book covers, and learning when to outsource the things I'm not very good at. I'm making measurable progress as I complete paragraph after paragraph, chapter after chapter. I'm gaining confidence in my research and writing skills. And I feel like the information I'll be providing eventual readers will help them lead happier lives. I've already decided the topic of my next book, because I know I won't get much happiness from the completion of this one. It's the process of researching, writing, and marketing that provides the real enjoyment.

Let's look at how to put this into effect as a teacher. Using the guidelines above, I choose a goal that is important to me and valued by society, is realistic and flexible, and is not materialistic. My third grade students are expected to know their multiplication facts up to 10 x 10 by memory. My goal can simply be that: All students will be able to answer 25 multiplication facts within 60 seconds by the end of the year.

I go into this goal knowing that I won't get much happiness from achieving it. If we succeed, I'll feel some momentary pride in the accomplishment, but there will be other goals, and in a few months I'll have a new class with which I'll have to start all over again.

I need not let that knowledge dampen my enthusiasm for striving toward the goal. I know that the real happiness will be found in the pursuit.

I'll need to investigate the best way to teach the facts. I'll learn things I didn't know before. I might find that singing songs is effective, and so I'll add singing multiplication fact songs to my morning routine, which the students will enjoy. I might enjoy it too. It'll add variety to my day. I might read an article about how damaging the focus on speed in math can be for some students and choose to alter my classroom practice accordingly. It might interest me so much that I decide to research the topic and learn even more. I might choose to share what I've learned in a blog post or even a book about practices that teachers should retire from their classrooms. I could have students track their own progress on the facts and share in their pride as they move closer to mastery. I'll take what I learn from this year's experience and apply it next year, thereby gaining competence in my craft. All of this will make me a happier teacher, and it comes from striving.

The science proves that tennis great Arthur Ashe was right when he said, "Success is a journey, not a destination. The doing is often more important than the outcome."

15. Have Fun

Take a moment to recall your clearest memories from your days as a student. Here are some of mine:

- A field trip to a maple syrup farm
- Building cells out of different kinds of candy
- Learning how to identify trees by walking around town during science class and studying their needles and leaves
- The time I gave an oral report on a book about Babe Ruth
- Playing a sports reporter while presenting a videotaped "newscast"
- The time I got in trouble for writing on the school's brick exterior with a hunk of ice
- The time I got in trouble for talking during a test
- Writing a book with a friend for the Young Authors contest
- Playing Jeopardy to review for tests
- An assembly with guys that were really good at throwing and catching Frisbees.

The reason I recall those moments with clarity and cannot recall 99 percent of my time in school is because they were outside the norm, and many of them triggered an emotional response. Most lessons and activities in classrooms don't elicit an emotional response from students. Those that do are memorable and are more likely to lead to real, lasting learning.

One indelible moment from elementary school was when I stood in front of the class to give an oral report on a biography I'd read about Babe Ruth. I was very shy when I was a kid and rarely spoke up in class. The idea of standing in front of 25 peers and talking while all of their eyes were on me was horrifying. While other students shared, I clenched my paper between my sweaty hands and read it over and over again. When I was done, the teacher told me I did a nice job, but reminded me that I was supposed to read an *autobiography*, not a biography. I remember this like it was yesterday because I was first terrified and then publicly embarrassed. On the other hand, I've never forgotten the difference between biographies and autobiographies.

Most of us don't want to terrify or embarrass our students so they can have a lasting memory of a classroom activity. We do, however, want them to remember what we've taught them. Few things make a teacher happier than when we run into a former student and they recall something they learned in our class. Fortunately, we don't have to traumatize kids to create these memories. We can simply make learning fun.

I bet you remember the field trips you went on as a child. You remember parts of every vacation you took with your family. You likely recall some of the assemblies you attended in school. You probably remember them better if they were fun. I remember building cells out of candy in science class, dissecting a frog, and learning about the digestive system by squeezing blended food through pantyhose because they were novel activities and fun to do.

A growing body of research suggests that fun can improve student performance by reducing anxiety, boosting participation, and increasing students' motivation to focus on the material. In one study, Sam Houston State University psychologist Randy Garner, PhD, found that students were more likely to recall a statistics lecture when it was interjected with jokes about relevant topics.[79]

A U.K. study of 700 participants showed that productivity increased an average of 12 percent and as high as 20 percent after viewing a comedy clip and enjoying some snacks and drinks. The report's author suggests showing a short film or some funny commercials before and during presentations.[80]

Humor is also one of the best remedies for stress. Like smiling, laughing reduces your level of stress hormones. Not only does it make you feel better, it also lowers your blood pressure, improves breathing, and regulates your heartbeat.

A 2005 University of Maryland study found that mental stress constricted blood vessels, leading to reduced blood flow. Since blood delivers oxygen to the brain and heart, this is kind of a big deal. Participants who watched a violent movie experienced a 35 percent reduction in blood flow. But those who watched a funny movie had 22 percent increased blood flow, which was equal to 15-30 minutes of exercise.[81]

While it's important to create compelling and memorable lessons for students, it's also important that teachers enjoy being at work. Teachers who like their jobs have more energy, work harder, get along better with others, and are more likely to stay with their current school. So having fun at work benefits both students and teachers.

In their book, *The Levity Effect,* Adrian Gostick and Scott Christopher write that, "People tend to remain with, stay committed to, and give more energy to an organization where good things are injected into work."[82]

A decade of research by the Great Place to Work Institute reveals the link between fun and outstanding work environments. Great companies consistently earn high marks for fun. Each year, GPWI asks tens of thousands of employees to rate their employer on a number of factors, including, "This is a fun place to work."

The Fortune 100 List of the Best Companies to Work For finds that great companies are places where people have fun. An average of 81 percent of surveyed employees say they are working in a fun environment at these companies. At merely good companies, only 62 percent report having fun.[83] Fortune doesn't list the worst companies, but if they did, I think it's safe to say that people there are not having a fabulous time.

Indeed, the chairwoman of the Institute says that it would be very unusual for a company to score high on the list and not score well on the fun question.[84]

Having more fun at school can be as simple as having a principal with a good sense of humor. Ipsos research found that employees who rated their manager's sense of humor above average rated the likelihood that they would be at the same job a year from now at almost 90 percent. Of those who rated their boss's sense of humor as average or worse, only 77 percent said they'd stay.[85] Gostick and Christopher write:

"An increasing body of research demonstrates that when leaders lighten up and create a fun workplace there's a significant increase in the level of employee trust, creativity,

and communication, leading to lower turnover, higher morale, and a stronger bottom line."[86]

Happy people perform better and want to stay where they are.

Leaders who have and encourage fun at work are more effective. Think about it: Who would you rather work for, a grump who never lightens up, or a leader who can loosen his tie, crack a joke, and allows his teachers to have fun? For which principal would you go the extra mile?

Your students are no different than you. They want a fun leader. You are their leader.

Physician and author Oliver Wendell Holmes once said, "We don't quit playing because we grow older; we grow older because we quit playing." In our quest for higher test scores and the resulting narrowing of the curriculum, too many schools have ignored our biological need to have fun. They do so at their peril. I fear that a kind of Matthew's Effect is happening to schools. Those labeled failing double-down on seriousness and push their students to meet higher expectations. They purchase test prep materials and require students to spend class time using them. They limit recess, cut extra-curricular opportunities from the school day, and say no to field trips. In short, they seriously curtail the fun students have.

Meanwhile, the affluent school on the other side of town, not fearful of low test results, is a place of low stress. Mixed in with serious learning are moments of levity. Teachers are more relaxed and have more fun with students. Administrators allow their staff members to be themselves. They have multiple field trips, regular assemblies, and students engage in fun, long-term projects. I can't prove it, but I'd be willing to bet this more relaxed and fun atmosphere contributes to higher test scores, rather than detracts from it. It's another case of the rich getting richer and the poor getting poorer.

While my most memorable school experiences triggered high-intensity emotions, they also stuck with me because they were different. Happy people recognize the importance of variety. We all experience habituation. We get used to things really quickly. Anything that doesn't change, even if it's really spectacular, gets taken for granted. Think of your cell phone. It's a technological marvel. People even ten years ago would not believe what your phone can do. And yet we get angry with it when a website loads slowly. In an interview with Conan O'Brien, comedian Louis CK uses his trademark wit to point out how ridiculous it is that we've all become used to something that should leave us in awe every time we experience it:

*"You're flying! It's amazing! Everybody on every plane should just constantly be going, 'Oh my God! Wow!' You're flying! You're sitting in **a chair in the sky**.*"[87]

So the sad reality is that if you went back to 1970 and showed someone everything your iPhone can do, they'd be amazed. For about a week. And then they'd wonder what the hell was wrong with the Netflix app.

Because we quickly adapt to even the most amazing things in our lives, we should embrace surprises. Happy people plan to change things up. They intentionally spice up their lives. They aren't afraid to take an occasional risk because they know it can enrich their existence. Variety is stimulating and produces longer-lasting happiness.

Not only do surprises themselves increase our happiness, but looking forward to something new and recalling enjoyable moments from the past also gives us joy. That's one reason why experiences provide more happiness than material goods.

A few years ago, my wife and I decided to surprise our Potterhead daughter with a spring break trip to The Wizarding World of Harry Potter at Universal Studios in Orlando. We planned it months in advance, which gave us lots of time to get excited about it. During stressful weeks at work, we would come home and talk about the trip. We got on the park's website and imagined what our daughter's reactions would be to the sites and rides. We reviewed our itinerary and talked about what Butterbeer might taste like and how we needed to get to Ollivander's early because our daughter would want her interactive wand the rest of the day. We downloaded an app that reported current wait times for the rides so we could identify the most popular ones. We mapped out a strategy for hitting those rides before the park got too full. We marinated in anticipation of the trip and extended the happiness the vacation provided by many months. In fact, research shows that we likely derived more joy from thinking about the Wizarding World than from actually going there.

A Dutch study found higher levels of reported happiness among vacationers who had yet to leave on their trips than non-vacationers, but no difference in happiness between the same groups following the trip, suggesting that it is the anticipation of a vacation that people most enjoy.[88] Research also concludes that people quickly return to their pre-trip levels of happiness following a vacation, even if the vacation was enjoyable and stress-free. The lesson for vacationers is to plan your trip well in advance to take advantage of this phenomenon.

You can do the same for fun events at school. Any change in routine can increase the fun for both you and your students. Be creative. Have kids make stuff. Try something out of left field. Once a month, do something with your students you've never done before. Change locations. Do a lesson outside, or in the gym or library. Volunteer your students to read at a nursing home. Do a service project like raking people's leaves or shoveling their walks. Plan a field trip and enjoy looking forward to it for months. Partner up with another class and have your students teach them something. Skype with an author whose books you've read or a scientist whose research you referenced in class. Have students participate in Genius Hour. Turn your room into a Makerspace. Try teaching a flipped lesson, or better yet, have your students teach one. Come up with a theme for the month, and have your students research and decorate the room. Throw a surprise party. The possibilities are endless and only bound by your imagination (and if you don't have one of those, ask your students for ideas, they have lots). Remember to let your students know about it ahead of time so they can benefit from the happiness they'll feel anticipating the big day.

Dale Carnegie said, "People rarely succeed unless they have fun in what they are doing." So crank up the fun at work, with or without your principal's consent, and you'll be happier, your students will be happier, you'll all be more productive, and your lessons will be more memorable.

16. Smile

A woman gets on a bus with her baby. The bus driver says: "Ugh, that's the ugliest baby I've ever seen!" The woman walks to the rear of the bus and sits down, fuming. She says to a man next to her: "The driver just insulted me!" The man says: "You go up there and tell him off. Go on, I'll hold your monkey for you."

When we smile, neuronal signals travel from the cortex of our brains to the brainstem. From there, the cranial muscle carries the signal further towards the smiling muscles in our face. These include the zygomatic major, a muscle in our cheeks, and the orbicularis oculi, which encircle our eyes. The presence of crow's feet at the corners of people's eyes are a sign of a genuine smile. Smiling produces endorphins, the same happy hormones you get from exercise. When you smile, a positive feedback loop is triggered. The smile tells your brain it feels good, and when your brain feels good it tells you to smile.

A genuine smile, what psychologists call a "Duchenne smile," is natural and universal. It can be distinguished from other smiles by nearly everyone. Even infants as young as 10 months will offer a false smile to an approaching stranger in contrast to the genuine Duchenne smile offered to the child's mother.[89] It is only this genuine Duchenne smile that activates both our cheek muscles and the muscles surrounding our eyes, and it's what researchers look for when determining authentic enjoyment.

Researchers have discovered that a lot of good things happen when we smile. British scientists found that one smile can provide the same level of brain stimulation as up to 2,000 chocolate bars.

University of California at Berkeley psychologists LeeAnne Harker and Dacher Keltner analyzed the college yearbook photos of women, then matched up their smile ratings with personality data collected during a 30-year longitudinal study. They found that women who displayed Duchenne smiles in their 21-year-old photo had greater levels of general well-being and marital satisfaction at age 52.[90] A related study, published in the April 2009 issue of the journal Motivation and Emotion, confirmed a relationship between low-intensity smiles in youth and divorce later in life.

Ernest Abel and Michael Kruger of Wayne State University wondered if smiling impacted our lifespans. In a 2010 study, they rated the smiles of professional baseball players captured in a 1952 yearbook, then determined each player's age at death. They found that smile intensity could explain 35 percent of the variability in survival. In any given year, players with Duchenne smiles in their yearbook photo were only half as likely to die as those without.[91]

Because the brain responds to the act of smiling in a positive way, we don't actually have to feel happy to smile. We can smile to feel happy. In one study, German researchers were able to induce happy feelings by having people clench a small pen between their teeth, imitating a smile. When the people held the pen in their protruding lips, imitating a pout, they felt unhappy.[92]

In a study from Kansas University, researchers found that participants who were instructed to smile, and in particular those whose faces expressed Duchenne smiles, had lower heart rates after recovery from stressful activities than those who held their faces in neutral expressions. This was true even for those volunteers who were told not to smile but held chopsticks in their mouths to force their face into a simulation of a smile.[93]

The researchers believe their findings suggest that smiling during brief periods of stress may help reduce the body's stress response, regardless of whether the person actually feels happy. So when one of your students gets under your skin or your principal announces a new initiative that stresses you out, finding a way to smile may be the best thing you can do.

Smiling will also benefit those around you, which may make your school a happier place to work. That's because smiling is contagious. Two Swedish studies from 2002 and 2011 confirmed that other people's smiles suppress the control we usually have over our facial muscles, compelling us to smile with them. This occurs even among strangers with whom we have no intention of making a connection. The reason humans do this is because mimicking a smile and experiencing it physically helps us interpret how genuine a person's smile is, so that we can understand their true emotional state.

A study by professors Nicholas Christakis and James Fowler found that when a person becomes happy, a friend living close by has a 25 percent higher chance of becoming happy themselves. A spouse experiences an 8 percent increased likelihood and for next-door neighbors, it's 34 percent.[94]

"Everyday interactions we have with other people are definitely contagious, in terms of happiness," says Christakis, the study's author.[95]

Perhaps more surprising is that the effect extends beyond the people we come into contact with. When one person becomes happy, the social network effect can spread up to three degrees, reaching friends of friends.

So it's true: Smile, and the world smiles with you.

This is great news for people who work in social environments like schools. Because kids smile about 400 times per day, and because smiling is contagious, and because feelings of happiness can spread like the flu virus in February, schools are poised to be very happy places.

And yet some of them aren't. A lot of teachers don't smile much at work. How can you smile more? First, stop taking yourself and your job so seriously. Yes, the work we do is important. Sure, we're important factors in our students' academic achievement. Okay, society, government, and possibly your administration like to scapegoat you for a multitude of problems this country faces. But the proper response to all of those things is not to be a grump. Being a hard-ass who never lightens up and cracks a smile at work won't make you a better teacher. And although the public likes to remind us how important we are, let's get some perspective. You teach kids. You don't negotiate peace treaties. Unlike doctors, it is highly unlikely you are going to save someone's life today. The chances are exceedingly slim that one of your "patients" is going to die under your care. It is absurd that teachers feel nearly as much stress on the job as doctors.

Almost all of a student's performance at school is based on factors outside of your control. Research by Dan Goldhaber and colleagues found that individual teacher differences account for just 8.5 percent of the variation in student achievement.[96] You are one of many teachers each student in your class will have over the course of their schooling. They will be influenced by all of those teachers, but most of them will be influenced far more by their family and the friends they choose. Once they leave you, they will have a great number of life experiences that will change them, experiences that we, and they, cannot even imagine. There is no question that you can make an impact. The testimonials of those who credit their teachers with inspiring them, believing in them, and challenging them prove it. You may very well change the lives of some of your students. But not most of them. Oprah may have been inspired by her fourth-grade teacher, but there were lots of other students Mrs. Duncan taught who remember her as just one in a long line of teachers they had.

Who will you blame if one of your students ends up in jail as an adult? When you hear of a heinous crime, do you immediately cast suspicion on the criminal's fifth grade teacher? Do you wonder how she could have let it happen? Conversely, when you read of someone's success, do you credit her 10th grade biology instructor or her kindergarten teacher? Not unless the successful person does. And thank goodness for that. I want to feel like I'm making a difference. In fact, a large part of the fulfillment I get from my job is feeling like the work I'm doing is consequential.

But that kind of thinking defies reality in most instances and for most students. It's a useful self-delusion that adds meaning to my work. But it can also be harmful. Because when we place this kind of emphasis on our jobs, it robs the student from receiving the credit or blame they themselves earn. And more importantly for the purposes of this book, all the pressure we put on ourselves to save every child — this belief that we and we alone are the critical factor that will determine whether a kid grows up to lead a rich life or ends up begging on a street corner — stresses teachers out, making them ultimately less effective, more prone to burning out, and more likely to quit, which means they won't be able to help any students.

Our inflated view of the impact we have might suffuse our work with purpose, but it can also destroy our happiness. We take ourselves too seriously and forget to enjoy our jobs. We scold kids for telling a genuinely funny joke because it derails our carefully planned lesson, instead of taking a moment to laugh along with him and his classmates. In our relentless quest to push our students to achieve, we forget the most human part of ourselves: the desire for happiness.

So how can we smile more and turn our schools into places of joy? First, if you're uncomfortable smiling, start your day by practicing in a mirror at home. Smiling is a skill, and like any skill, it can be improved with practice. Try to get those crow's feet to appear at the corners of your eyes. To help you, recall some of the funniest moments from your life.

Start your workday by smiling at everyone you meet. Most teachers have some running around to do in the morning before students arrive. Smile and say good morning to everyone, even that old sourpuss Joyce who never smiles at anyone. Challenge yourself to get her to return your smile. Be overly cheerful around her. Be obnoxiously positive. It will be a measure of your growing competency if you can get Joyce to break into a grin.

Greet all of your students with that same smile when they enter your room in the morning. I stand outside my room and try to greet most of mine by name. I offer handshakes and smiles. The message I send is that we get to choose which attitude to have every single morning. You determine how you carry yourself. You can choose to be energetic, and you get to decide how to greet others every morning. To those students who had a rough day the day before, I want them to understand that I'm not holding a grudge. Every day in my room is a fresh start, and I'm happy that they're there.

If we want positive, energetic students, we have to model that behavior first thing in the morning.

Look for the humor in every situation. We've all sat through infuriating staff meetings. I used to get worked up with what I felt was the wrongheadedness of some district initiatives and speak my mind. Now that I've been with my district for more years that I care to admit, I often find myself amused by the things that used to infuriate me. Some decisions are so dumb, the only thing to do is smile.

We've all had class clowns on our roster. Most of the time, they're not actually amusing and are more annoying than anything, both to us and their classmates. But every once in awhile, they say or do something that's legitimately funny. You have to be able to smile or even laugh at these moments. Show your human side. Don't hold the kid's past against him. Give him the gift of your laughter. You may just find he's more willing to listen to you when you allow yourself to be seen as a real person with an actual sense of humor. Comedian Jim Carrey constantly disrupted class when he was a kid because he found that humor made him likeable. Most teachers punished him and wrote critical remarks on his report cards.

But one was smart enough to cut a deal. She told him that if he could sit quietly and do his work all day, then she would give him the last few minutes to entertain the class. She had much better success than those who stifled and attempted to change his personality.

You could also watch funny videos with your students during breaks. There's nothing wrong with having movement breaks for your students. Research supports their use. But how about, every once in awhile, you take a humor break? Since you now know the benefits of smiling, you can justify, both to yourself and to your principal, the showing of a funny YouTube clip between lessons, or you could allow kids to come to the front of the room to tell their favorite jokes.

And speaking of jokes, why not share a few of your own? The most popular books in my classroom library are easily the funny ones. *Diary of a Wimpy Kid*, *Captain Underpants*, and joke books are always in heavy rotation with my students. Kids of all ages love to laugh. If you ever need to quickly gain their attention, say the words, "I have a joke to tell you." Then actually tell them one. If you're not a natural joke-teller, start by memorizing a few funny ones. Here's one I like:

Why do ducks have flat feet? To stamp out forest fires.
Why do elephants have flat feet? To stamp out flaming ducks.

And here's one you probably shouldn't share in class. It's just for you:

I went to the zoo the other day. There was only one dog in it. It was a shih tzu.

17. Make Their Day

The mother had recently received medical treatment that left her feet numb and sensitive to pressure. Most of her shoes were now completely useless. Her daughter logged onto the Zappos website and ordered her mom six pairs of shoes in the hope that at least one of them would be comfortable enough for her to wear. After the shoes arrived, the mother called Zappos to ask how she could return the shoes she didn't want. She felt compelled to explain why she was returning so many shoes.

Two days later, a large bouquet of flowers was delivered to her door. The attached card wished her well and hoped she would soon recover from her treatment. It was from Zappos. The online shoe retailer, famous for its excellent customer service, also upgraded the mother and daughter to VIP Members, which entitled them to free expedited shipping on all orders.[97]

This is just one of many stories you can find about Zappos' superb customer service. It isn't an accident or the result of a few thoughtful people at the company.

In a Harvard Business Review article from 2010, Zappos CEO Tony Hsieh explains how the company views every interaction with a customer as an opportunity to create an emotional impact and a lasting memory. They offer free shipping both ways. Customers can send back shoes for any reason at no charge. They have a 365-day return policy (for shoes!). Their website lists their customer service phone number prominently on every page, whereas most bury it so deep only a determined customer can find it. Their call center is staffed 24 hours a day, seven days a week.[98]

That call center is located in Las Vegas. Customer service representatives are paid $11 an hour, just a couple of bucks more than minimum wage. But Zappos has no trouble finding people to answer their phones. In one recent year, 25,000 people applied for a job. Only 250 were hired. Statistically, it was easier to get accepted into Harvard than it was to get hired by Zappos, where you earn eleven bucks an hour to answer questions about shoes.

Why would so many people want to work for Zappos? The company has some nice perks, such as generous insurance packages, free food at work, and a 40 percent employee discount off their merchandise. But lots of companies offer similar benefits and don't regularly make Forbes' list of best companies to work for. What Zappos really offers their employees is a chance to help other people. The CEO explains:

"At Zappos we don't hold reps accountable for call times. (Our longest phone call, from a customer who wanted the rep's help while she looked at what seemed like thousands of pairs of shoes, lasted almost six hours.) And we don't upsell—a practice that usually just annoys customers. We care only whether the rep goes above and beyond for every customer. We don't have scripts, because we want our reps to let their true personalities shine during every phone call, so that they can develop a personal emotional connection with each customer."[99]

Zappos employees love working for the company because they're trusted to make decisions and because they help people all day long. In his book *Flourish*, Martin Seligman says, "We scientists have found that doing a kindness produces the single most reliable momentary increase in well-being of any exercise we have tested."[100]

Performing acts of kindness has been shown to boost energy. Nearly 50 percent of participants in one study reported feeling stronger and more energetic after helping others. Many also reported feeling calmer, with increased perceptions of self-worth.[101]

The performing of kind acts stimulates our brains' pleasure centers by increasing dopamine levels. According to research from Emory University, when you are kind to others your brain's reward centers light up. The phenomenon is nicknamed the "helper's high."

Being kind to others also lowers stress, reduces depression, and makes us happier. Consistently kind people have 23 percent less of the stress hormone cortisol, and they age slower than more selfish people. Kindness stimulates the production of serotonin and endorphins. These chemicals help to heal wounds, lead to feelings of serenity, boost happiness, and act as a natural painkiller.

Kindness improves relationships. People like people who are kind. They feel a closer connection to them. Scientists believe we're wired this way. It makes sense; our evolutionary ancestors had to cooperate in order to survive. These "kindness genes" were passed down to us today, which is why when we are kind we feel a stronger connection to people, new relationships are forged, and existing ones are strengthened.

Kindness also improves our health and leads to longer lives. People who volunteer tend to experience fewer aches and pains. Helping others protects overall health as much as aspirin protects against heart disease. Acts of kindness can produce oxytocin, which causes the release of nitric oxide in blood vessels. Nitric oxide dilates our blood vessels, thereby reducing blood pressure. People 55 and older who volunteer at two or more organizations have a 44 percent lower likelihood of dying early, even after other contributing factors are removed.[102] This is a stronger effect than exercising four times per week.

Like smiling, kindness is contagious. Acts of kindness ripple outwards, like a stone dropped in a pond, touching others' lives and inspiring more kindness everywhere the wave goes. One study reported on an anonymous 28-year-old person who walked into a clinic and donated a kidney. It set off a 'pay it forward' effect where the spouses or other family members of recipients of a kidney donated one of theirs to someone else in need. The 'domino effect', as it was called in the New England Journal of Medicine report, spanned the U.S. Ten people received a new kidney as a consequence of that anonymous donor.[103]

The positive effects of kindness are experienced in the brain of everyone who witnesses the act, improving their mood and making them more likely to do a kindness of their own. This means one good deed in a crowded area or shared on social media can create a kindness snowball that can improve the days of dozens of people!

Science has a few things to say about the best ways to be kind. Smaller acts tend to provide more happiness than larger ones. While doing something big to help another person is a good thing, small, frequent acts of kindness will do more for your long-term happiness. Variety helps too. Performing a wide array of kind acts helps maximize our happiness, whereas repeatedly doing the same act of kindness may lose its effectiveness. One study showed that subjective happiness was increased simply by counting one's acts of kindness for a week.[104]

If you really want to make someone's day, do something they don't expect. A compliment can go a long way. Most of us think positive things about people but never tell them. You can also do something extra and unexpected. There's a reason wives love getting flowers from their husbands: It doesn't happen very often, and it shows that the husband was thinking about his wife. It's an unexpected act of kindness.

I have a terrible memory and forget most things, but I remember a waitress I had at a Fuddruckers when I was a freshman in high school. Male freshmen are about as far down on the pecking order as can be. All the girls who just last year you had a shot with are now dating upperclassmen. You're gawky and immature. Your face is pimply. You don't know much of anything. You can't drive yet. There's just nothing good about being a male freshman. So when that waitress took my order and said, "You have beautiful eyelashes," it was something that surprised me and made me feel better about myself.

We all notice things we like about other people: a bubbly personality, a bright smile, an outfit, a new hair style. But because we're worried that our compliment could be misinterpreted — seen as flirty or somehow inappropriate — we don't say anything at all. Think about it from the receiving end. How many times have you been offended by a genuine compliment? I never have been. I always appreciate them. We should tell others when we notice something good about them. It will make them happier, and it will do the same for us.

An unexpected act of kindness can last far into the future. It can even change history. As a teacher, one of the greatest kindnesses you can perform is to see something in a student when there really isn't anything to see. My favorite example is Thomas Edison's mother. Edison was a restless and awful student for the short time he attended school. He described the episode that ended his formal schooling in an interview published in *T.P.'s Weekly* in 1907.

"One day I overheard the teacher tell the inspector that I was "addled" and it would not be worthwhile keeping me in school any longer. I was so hurt by this last straw that I burst out crying and went home and told my mother about it. Then I found out what a good thing a good mother is. She came out as my strong defender. Mother love was aroused, mother pride wounded to the quick. She brought me back to the school and angrily told the teacher that he didn't know what he was talking about, that I had more brains than he himself, and a lot more talk like that. In fact, she was the most enthusiastic champion a boy ever had, and I determined right then that I would be worthy of her and show her that her confidence was not misplaced."[105]

My own story involves my eighth grade gym teacher, Mr. Robinson. Like most boys, I wanted to be a professional athlete. First baseball, then basketball. The problem was I wasn't very good at either. There were probably ten kids in my eighth grade class who were better athletes than I was. I was flat-out terrible at a number of the activities we did in gym class. I hated gymnastics. I had zero upper body strength, so I got destroyed during the wrestling unit. I couldn't climb the rope that hung from a ceiling beam. I could only do about five pull-ups and ten push-ups. And yet, when it was time for the end-of-the-year awards ceremony, Mr. Robinson presented me with the Gym Student of the Year. I still have no idea why. I knew I didn't deserve it. But somehow that didn't matter. I suddenly had a different self-image. I saw myself as an athlete, simply because my teacher did. I believed in myself, and that belief led me to work harder at basketball. By my senior year, I was a starter on a team that went 22-3 and made it to the quarterfinals of the state tournament, and I had made the Honorable Mention list for the all-conference team.

What a gift it is to see something in someone that they don't yet see in themselves.

As teachers, we have the chance to do this every day. You may never know where that surprising kindness will lead, but you can be sure that your own happiness will increase as a result of doing it.

The power of surprising kindness is the secret behind Zappos' success. Nobody expects even average customer service these days, so when Zappos goes above and beyond to help their customers, those customers are shocked, grateful, and very happy.

Outstanding customer service, a form of kindness, has lasting effects. Zappos knows that a happy customer will return, again and again, to buy more shoes from them instead of a competitor. They know that happy customers will tell others about their experience. Think how many new customers Zappos has gotten over the years as stories like the one you read at the start of this chapter spread.

Zappos also benefits from having happier employees. Because acts of kindness provide many benefits for those who perform them, Zappos workers love their jobs. Because they love their jobs, they do them better. And because they tell others about how great their jobs are, the company receives many more applicants every year than they could possibly hire, meaning they get to choose from the very best and hire only those people who will perpetuate their culture of great customer service.

You can, and should, apply all of those lessons to your job as a teacher. If you are consistently kind to your students you will be known, like Zappos, as a teacher who provides outstanding customer service. Students will like being in your class. They will look forward to coming and will behave better when there. They will tell other students about you. Those students will tell their parents. They'll talk about how much they like school. Some of them will have had bad experiences in previous years and by comparison, you will stand out. Students in lower grades will want to be in your room. They will like you before they even know you. They'll know who you are, wave to you in the hallway, and shout your name across the playground. Who doesn't want to be treated with kindness, after all?

When June rolls around and thoughts turn to next year, those students will tell their parents that they want you for their teacher. Some of those parents — the involved ones who tend to raise better students — will request you for their child's teacher. Your class will end up with kids who want to be there, parents who want their kids there, and you getting the benefit of every doubt. You will start each year with many built-in advantages.

If you provide great customer service year after year, you'll establish a reputation that will make your job less stressful and go a long way toward making you a happier teacher.

Like the other strategies in this book you can use to increase your own happiness, you can pass this one on to your students. One school in the district where I work does something they call Positive Post-It Day. Students throughout the school go around and stick Post-it notes on lockers with messages that convey appreciation, thanks, compliments, or simply kind words.

Inspired by a touching true story written by Sister Helen Mrosla, many teachers ask students to write the best thing they can say about each student in their class. The papers are collected, and the teacher compiles lists of compliments for each student to keep.[106] Many students report savings these lists for years to come.

The Random Acts of Kindness Foundation has a great website for teachers that includes lessons, videos, and kindness ideas. A simple Google search or visit to Pinterest will give you many more ideas on how you can teach students the value of kindness. There are also plenty of YouTube videos showing random acts of kindness among strangers. Viewing them with students is an effective way to counter the many negative images they receive about human nature from the media.

Of course, the best way to teach kindness is the best way to teach just about everything: model it. Don't be a jerk. Be nice as often as you possibly can. Provide exceptional customer service. It won't happen overnight, but over the course of the year you will set a powerful example for your students about how people should treat others.

18. Get Recognized

You may have never heard of Yum! Brands, but you have surely eaten at one of their restaurants. A Fortune 500 company, Yum! Brands employs 1.5 million people in 120 countries around the world. It is the largest fast food company on the planet and operates all Pizza Hut, Taco Bell, KFC, and Wingstreet brands.

Until recently, Yum! Brands was run by CEO David Novak. Novak believes that the key to business success is putting people first. His epiphany came when he was Chief Operating Officer at Pepsico.

"I loved going out to the bottling plants. I'd get in at six in the morning, I would meet with route salesman and merchandisers and ask what's working, what's not working. One time I was in St. Louis...and everyone started raving about Bob. They described how he was the best merchandiser in the company. I looked down at the end of the table and Bob is crying...He said, 'I've been in this company for 47 years and I never knew people felt this way about me.'"[107]

Novak couldn't believe that Bob never knew how much he was appreciated. At that moment Novak decided to become a master at recognizing his employees. While leading KFC, he would reward deserving workers with a signed and numbered rubber chicken—along with a $100 on-the-spot bonus. Novak would take a picture with the "floppy chicken" winner and hang it in his office.

His managers at Yum! Brands rewarded workers with sets of chattering teeth on legs, a symbolic gesture for those who upheld company values, or "walked the talk." He's also given out sauce packets and cheese-shaped hats to top employees.

Novak's strategy of recognizing people worked. From 1997 to 2013, Yum! Brands outperformed the S&P 500 by an average of 12 percent per year. If you had invested $1,000 in Yum! Brands' stock in 1997, it would have been worth about $6,500 by 2013. The same $1,000 invested in the S&P 500 over the same period would have grown to only $1,850. During Novak's tenure as CEO, Yum! Brands doubled in size and became a global powerhouse, going from approximately 20 percent of its profits coming from outside the U.S. in 1997 to nearly 70 percent in 2014.

Novak says, "The key to achieving the perfect company is putting your people first. Recognition is a secret weapon that every leader really needs to use."[108]

As teachers, we know all about Abraham Maslow and his hierarchy of needs. At the bottom of his ubiquitous triangle are basic survival needs like food and air. Above that, people need safety. Once that need is met, humans require feelings of love and belonging to thrive. After that comes self-esteem. To be at our best, we need to feel competent and confident. We need to achieve, to master, and to make progress toward our goals. And we need to feel respected by others and have our accomplishments recognized.

People crave positive feedback, recognition that they put in extra effort, acknowledgement from both leaders and peers, and the glow that comes with knowing an achievement has been seen, appreciated, and celebrated. People need more than constructive feedback and nonspecific affirmation. They need recognition for going above and beyond. This will never go away as a basic human need.

Recognition and praise are two critical components for creating positive emotions in organizations. Gallup surveyed more than four million employees worldwide on this topic. Their analysis found that individuals who received regular recognition and praise:

- increased their productivity
- increased engagement with colleagues
- were more likely to stay with their organization
- received higher loyalty and satisfaction scores from customers[109]

The majority of us don't give or receive anywhere near the amount of recognition we should. As a result, we're less productive, and in many cases, completely disengaged at work. According to the U.S. Department of Labor, the number one reason people leave their jobs is because they "do not feel appreciated."[110]

Now Superintendent of the Racine Unified School District in Racine, Wisconsin, Dr. Lolli Haws understood this in her previous job as a principal: "I learned that recognizing teachers is a critically important part of my job, since teaching can sometimes feel like an unappreciated effort day in and day out," she says. "Recognition from adults for a job well done or appreciation of ongoing efforts is vital."[111]

And yet, only 17 percent of employees who participated in a Bersin & Associates study indicated that their organizations' cultures strongly supported recognition. Most recognition programs were misguided. 87 percent of organizations reported that their programs were designed to recognize service or tenure, a vestige of the days when unions required employers to recognize longevity. Programs like these do not meet the needs of today's employees, nearly 70 percent of whom report they are recognized annually or not at all.[112] Simply put, recognizing someone once a year for doing nothing more than hanging around isn't very effective.

The research shows that for employees, the most important elements of a recognition program are the ability to receive specific feedback and to give recognition easily. In fact, the top reason employees do not recognize each other is because there is no established way to do so. Districts have a responsibility to put recognition programs in place for teachers to recognize the good work their colleagues do.

When I reached the fifteen-year mark of my teaching career, I was called up to the stage at a welcome back assembly and handed a pin emblazoned with the logo of my teachers' union. I have no idea where this pin is today. I never wore it or even took it out of the plastic it came in. I had done nothing to earn it other than return year after year. On the other hand, I've saved every single handwritten thank you card given to me by principals and parents. I'm not alone, either. One survey found that 76 percent of people save these cards.[113] Like David Novak's rubber chickens and chattering teeth, we earned those.

According to a recent OGO survey, 82 percent of employed Americans don't feel that their supervisors recognize them enough for their contributions.[114] This lack of recognition takes a toll on morale, productivity, and, ultimately, success. 40

percent of Americans say they'd put more energy into their work if they were recognized more.[115] My suspicion is that schools are even worse than business when it comes to recognizing employees. Teachers are often seen as selfless people who are there for their students and who don't really need to be recognized.

A lack of funds also contributes. Some principals, knowing there's no money for extras, give up on recognition altogether, not realizing that many teachers would appreciate many of the no-cost options listed later in this chapter just as much as a T-shirt, gift card, fancy pen, or bonus check.

Because business has started to recognize the importance of recognition for employee happiness, productivity, and profitability, a lot of research has gone into how to do it effectively. Most experts believe recognition should be based on specific results and behaviors. Don't give a general Employee of the Month award. Instead, give an award for solving a particular problem or reaching a specific goal with students. This can create a culture of values, where awards are given only for those things that matter most to the organization.

Teacher-to-teacher recognition beats principal-to-teacher recognition. Being noticed by our boss has less impact than we think. Other teachers have a better grasp of the challenges of the job and what we're going through on a day-to-day basis, so when they thank us for our efforts, the impact is more meaningful. Recognition from a principal can be perceived as political, and quiet, introverted high performers who do great, but less public work, often go unnoticed.

A powerful way to recognize teachers is through storytelling. When a teacher does something beyond the call of duty or has great success with students on a critical goal, they should be recognized, and we should tell others about it. Mention them in a district-wide newsletter or highlight their accomplishment on the district website or Facebook page. Invite the local newspaper to do a story on it. Take a photo of the teacher, write a caption describing her accomplishment, and display it in a school showcase.

The offices of Yum! Brands are devoid of any corporate art. Instead, the walls and even parts of the ceiling are festooned with photographs of the CEO recognizing his employees. While this kind of storytelling has proven benefits, it's not for everyone. Good principals will know their staff and avoid public displays for those teachers who prefer quieter recognition.

Recognition should be easy to do and frequent. Once a year won't do it. Teachers do hard jobs, and much of their best work is witnessed by no one other than their students, who often don't understand or appreciate it. If we hope for teachers to recognize their colleagues' efforts, teachers can't view doing so as a chore to add to their long list of other tasks. Long forms to fill out, essays that require paragraphs of supporting evidence, and processes that require the approval of administrators will lead to less recognition. Make the process as simple and transparent as possible, and more teachers will benefit from feeling valued at work.

While the above recommendations are all research-based, perhaps the best thing to do is survey your employees about the ways they'd like to be recognized. Every person is different. Some want showy displays that let everyone know about their great work. Others prefer a discreet thank you card slipped into their mailbox. One company has every new employee fill out an orientation survey on their first day. One of the questions asked is, "Tell us about a time you felt appreciated for your work."[116]

Ideally, school districts will initiate recognition programs that follow the best practices mentioned above. Principals will be important players in this process as they make teachers aware of it, encourage participation, and occasionally recognize teachers for their efforts.

Principals need not spend much money to effectively recognize staff members. Handwritten thank you cards cost nearly nothing, they take little time to write, and a copy of them can be made to help principals when composing teacher evaluations at the end of the year. Principals can also give the gift of time. No teacher ever has enough time, and everyone appreciates a break. Principals can take over a class for a special read-aloud. They can take over a teacher's recess or bus duty as a token of thanks for a job well done. They can allow a teacher to go home an hour early while they take over the teacher's responsibilities. None of these cost the district money, but they would all be greatly appreciated by every teacher I know.

Principals could also declare a special day to reward staff for progress toward a meaningful school goal. A random Tuesday could become a "Jeans Day," where teachers can dress more casually. Teachers could be rewarded with an extra 30 minutes of lunch while students are kept in the gym and shown a movie or given an extra recess.

Acknowledgement of teachers' talents is also a form of recognition. If a particular teacher excels in a certain area, ask that teacher to share their expertise at a staff meeting or upcoming professional development day.

Finally, administrators can steal a page from business executives like David Novak. Go out and buy something silly, like a stuffed animal of your school's mascot or a huge plush apple, and present this to teachers at staff meetings so they can proudly display it in their classrooms for a week.

Unfortunately, not all administrators are aware of the research on the importance of recognition. Since it's so important to your happiness, you shouldn't wait around for your district or principal to recognize your good work. Ask to start staff meetings with five minutes of recognition, and have teachers share positives from the classroom. Come up with a token of recognition that will stay in a teacher's room for a week. If administrators want no part of it, go around them and have teachers nominate other teachers via email every Friday. Ask to have teachers and their students recognized over PA announcements each morning or afternoon. Buy a large package of cheap thank you cards and give 20 to every teacher. Set a goal of everyone using them to thank one another by the end of the semester. Develop a culture of appreciation at your school.

When all else fails, don't be afraid to self-promote. The teachers who are considered the best in a school and community are often the ones who aren't afraid to sell themselves. Post about your successes on your class website or Facebook page. Write about your accomplishments in your classroom newsletter that you send to parents. Start a blog where you document the great things you're doing, and highlight your students' achievements.

A lot teachers won't do this. It's immodest. It's self-aggrandizing. We're not supposed to be self-promoters. It feels too "markety." Get over it. Think about "famous" teachers like Rafe Esquith, Ron Clark, Michelle Rhee, Deborah Meier, Colby Sharp, Donalyn Miller, Dave Burgess, and Pernille Ripp. They're famous not because they're great teachers (they might be, but I've never seen any of them teach), but because they self-promote. Almost all of them write books, are active on social media, and/or do public speaking engagements. They branched out from teaching in some way. They got themselves known, and because they are known, everyone assumes they must be excellent educators. They all receive frequent, positive recognition because they're noticed. Getting recognized is important for your happiness at work, so if you're not getting it, take action.

19. Forgive

"Holding on to anger is like grasping a hot coal with the intent of throwing it at someone else; you are the one getting burned." -Buddha

In 2012, 14-year-old Jordan Howe was being bullied at school, and fearing escalation, he brought his father's gun with him. He took it out on the bus to show his friends and accidentally shot 13-year-old Lourdes Guzman-DeJesus in the neck, killing her. Instead of holding on to anger, the girl's mother, Ady Guzman-DeJesus, not only forgave her daughter's killer, but she pushed for and approved a lighter sentence that included him touring schools with her to warn children of the dangers of gun violence. Said the judge, "In the 20 years I've watched human tragedy unfold in this courtroom, I could have never imagined a victim's mother embracing her child's killer."[117]

Ady Guzman-DeJesus knew, without reading any scientific studies, the power of forgiveness. She and many others innately understand the lesson behind Buddha's quote: That holding on to hatred ultimately hurts the victim more than the offender. While Jordan Howe didn't deserve forgiveness, he was granted it anyway, not to absolve him of his actions, but because Ady Guzman-DeJesus knew it was the only way to heal herself.

When you forgive someone, you make the choice to give up your desire for revenge and feelings of resentment. You also stop judging the person who caused you the hurt. Instead of revenge, resentment, and judgment, you show generosity, compassion, and kindness. In forgiveness, you don't forget that the offense occurred, nor do you excuse it. You substitute your negative with positive feelings, thoughts, and behavior.[118]

Research has shown that forgiveness provides us with a number of benefits. It is associated with better health in terms of our hearts, hormones, and immune systems, and also provides psychological benefits.

People who forgive are less likely to be depressed and anxious, and more likely to be happy.

In one study, participants were asked to think about someone who had mistreated them. While they thought about this person and his or her past offense, their blood pressure, heart rate, facial muscle tension, and sweat gland activity all increased. Thinking about their grudges was stressful, and subjects found the recollections unpleasant. It made them feel angry, sad, anxious, and less in control. Participants were also asked to try to empathize with their offenders or imagine forgiving them. While doing so, their physical arousal fell. They showed no more of a stress reaction than normal wakefulness produces.[119]

Toussaint and colleagues found a significant relationship between forgiving others and positive health among middle-aged and older Americans. People over 45 who had forgiven others reported greater satisfaction with their lives and were less likely to report symptoms of psychological distress, such as feelings of nervousness, restlessness, and sadness.[120]

If you want to profit from the life-extending benefits of forgiveness, don't wait for others to apologize to you or to promise that they will change. Start the process within your own mind, and you'll be happier and live longer.

Forgiveness benefits you, and it also helps your students. When we forgive students, we treat their transgressions as mistakes instead of evidence of poor character. We send the message that we're not happy with their choices, but we still like them and believe in them as people. Who doesn't appreciate the chance to start again?

Forgiveness comes from empathy. Seek to understand where the student is coming from. I have had students in the past who were real challenges in the classroom. I'd get frustrated with their behavior and wonder why they acted so poorly. Then I'd have a conference with the student's parents and my perspective would completely change. After some of these meetings, I'd wonder how they were able to hold it together as well as they did at school.

The reason Ady Guzman-DeJesus was able to forgive Jordan Howe was empathy. At one of the school visits Howe and Guzman-DeJesus did to teach students about the dangers of gun violence, a student asked Guzman-DeJesus how she stopped wanting harsh prison time for Jordan. "What was the turning point?" the student asked.

Guzman-DeJesus said, "I know he didn't do it on purpose. It took me awhile to understand that. He's not a killer. I know in his heart, he's sorry. I decided to forgive him."[121] Empathy. Understanding. Seeing things from a different, and more compassionate, perspective. Those are the keys to forgiveness.

It's easier said than done. One trick I use to forgive others is to remind myself of my own frequent screw-ups. I make some of the same mistakes my students do, and I'm a lot older. For example, every morning my students are supposed to choose which lunch they will be having: A choice, B choice, or cold. They move a magnet to indicate their selection. Most days, a student or two will forget to do this simple task. It drives me nuts, especially in April when they've been doing it for eight months. How can they not remember to pick a lunch? We practice and practice the morning routine at the start of the year. I've explained how their failure to pick a lunch messes up my routine of marking the lunches and taking attendance. What's the matter with them? How can they forget?

And then, often the same day, I am reminded of my hypocrisy when the office has to call down and remind me to take attendance. How could I forget?

It happens at home, too. I get upset with my daughter for forgetting things. Some days, she leaves the house and gets into the car without her backpack! I tell her very adult things like, "You have to think before you leave the house." It's a good thing she doesn't know that so far this year I've forgotten to take my lunch to work seven times. The truth is that many of us are much quicker to forgive ourselves than we are to forgive others. By admitting our own faults, it's easier to forgive others' theirs.

A second mental exercise to try is to ask, "Whose fault is it, really?" I'm currently reading an old Judy Blume novel, *Iggie's House,* with a group of third graders. The story is about housing discrimination in the 1960s. There's a young girl in it named Clarice Landon, who, like her prejudiced mother, wants nothing to do with the black family that has moved into their white neighborhood. One of the questions we discuss as a class is, "Is Clarice to blame for the way she acts?" Most of the class thinks she isn't. She's only 11, after all. The kids blame her mother. I then ask, "At what age *will* she be to blame?" To this question, I get many answers, and it leads to a very interesting conversation. I don't know what that age is either, but I am sure that the students in front of us aren't usually at fault for the way they act. People generally behave the only way they know how. If you put yourself in their shoes — if you had their parents, and went home to live in their houses every night, and you had their experiences — would you really act any differently?

When you're trying to get better at forgiving people, it helps to see things from their point of view.

That's not to say that you accept or ignore poor behavior. You're a teacher, and one thing you teach is self-discipline. That's why you have a classroom management plan. Your role is to play referee. When students break a rule, make the call, and give your predetermined consequence. There's no need to make it personal and no reason to hold it against them. Everybody hates the referee that holds an obvious grudge against a player or team. We see that referee as unfair. It's no different for teachers.

Seek to understand your students and then empathize with them. Many of them are going through things we can't imagine. Forgive them. Then patiently teach them how to make better choices while never backing down from holding them accountable for the choices they're making now. When you dispassionately apply the consequences outlined in your classroom management plan, you let students know you believe in their ability to improve. Be kind, be positive, start each day over with a smile and a handshake, and end each day the same way. Forgive, and you and your students will be happier.

20. Nurture Relationships

If you do nothing else to enhance your happiness, make sure you cultivate the relationships you have with the most important people in your life. Social connection is one of our fundamental human needs. We are wired to love and be loved. We have a strong urge to belong. When you think about most of the things that people strive for — money, power, fame, beauty — the root of every one of those desires is a powerful need to be accepted, admired, and even adored by others.

People with strong social ties have lower rates of anxiety and depression. Studies show they also have higher self-esteem, are more empathic, trust and cooperate better with others, and benefit from higher trust and collaboration from other people.

It is quality, not quantity, that matters when it comes to your friends. You need between three and five close confidants for optimal well-being, suggests research from Dr. Robin Dunbar, an psychologist at the University of Oxford. But even one very good friend can improve your life in profound ways.

Kahneman and others used something called the Day Reconstruction Method to determine how 909 employed women rated the activities of their day. Socializing ranked second, behind only sex, and ahead of relaxing, eating, watching TV, and shopping. The survey also found that participants preferred socializing with friends and family to interacting with clients, co-workers, or their boss. But any social interaction was preferable to being alone.[122]

I recently had to get out of the house. It was a Sunday, and I wanted to watch a basketball game and drink a beer. My wife didn't want to go, so I called a friend, but he was unavailable. I decided to go anyway. I went to one of my favorite restaurants, a place at which I'd had a number of good times in the past. I sat at the bar, drank my beer, and watched the first half of the game. I spoke only to the bartender because there was no one sitting near me. It was boring, no fun at all. On the other hand, I've had a great time doing nothing but riding in a car with three of my favorite people.

Most people don't go to movies alone. Apart from the social stigma, they know that it's just not as fun to watch a movie by yourself, even though you're unlikely to talk much to the person you're with while the film is playing. We're social people. We yearn to be in the company of people we like. If you made a scrapbook of the greatest moments of your life, the scrapbook would be filled with things you did in the company of family and friends.

The need for social connection is so strong that simply thinking of loved ones can make us happier. In fact, researchers from Carnegie Mellon University have found that significant interactions with Facebook friends can bolster users' reported well-being, with effects comparable in size to those of major life events. Researchers Moira Burke and Robert Kraut found that genuine, personalized interactions from real friends, such as commenting on another's post or writing on a friend's wall, are a significant form of social engagement. "People derive benefits from online communication, as long it comes from others they care about and has been tailored for them," the authors write.[123]

In an experiment by Paul Zak, a neuroeconomist from California with the slightly disturbing moniker "Dr. Love," a journalist had his level of oxytocin, the hormone responsible for feelings of happiness, measured while using Twitter. The journalist's oxytocin levels spiked 13.2 percent, the equivalent of a hormonal spike experienced by a groom on his wedding day whose oxytocin levels Zak had measured previously. Meanwhile, the journalist's stress hormones went down 10.8 percent and 14.9 percent, respectively. Explained Zak to his subject: "Your brain interpreted tweeting as if you were directly interacting with people you cared about or had empathy for. E-connection is processed in the brain like an in-person connection."[124]

Zak's research has led him to conclude: "If I'm a totally selfish person and I want to maximize my own happiness, I've got to reach out. I've got to go volunteer, I've got to help other people. I've got to engage with others."[125]

For those who question the importance of social connection, consider the sting of rejection. A brain imaging study led by Ethan Kross at the University of Michigan suggests that the same parts of the brain are activated during social rejection as during physical pain.[126] We have a need to feel accepted, and when that need goes unfulfilled, or we fear that it might, we suffer because of it. To put it in more concrete terms, that student playing by herself on the playground because no one will play with her is suffering as though she has been punched in the stomach.

Despite its clear connection to our happiness, research suggests that social connectedness is falling in the U.S. One study showed that the modal number of people with whom one felt comfortable sharing a personal problem dropped from three in 1985 to just one in 2004. One in four Americans said they had *no one* to confide in.[127]

This may explain why increasing numbers of people are reporting loneliness, isolation, and alienation, and why Americans are more depressed than they've been in decades.[128] Those who are not socially connected are more likely to experience anxiety, depression, antisocial behavior, and even suicidal thoughts.

A landmark survey showed that a lack of social connectedness predicts vulnerability to disease and death, above and beyond traditional risk factors such as smoking, blood pressure, and physical activity. As a predictor of early death, loneliness eclipses obesity. In his research, professor John Cacioppo has shown that loneliness affects several key bodily functions, at least in part through overstimulation of the body's stress response. Chronic loneliness is associated with increased levels of cortisol, a major stress hormone, as well as higher vascular resistance, which can raise blood pressure and decrease blood flow to vital organs.

Professor Cacioppo's research has also shown that the danger signals activated in the brain by loneliness affect the production of white blood cells, which can impair the immune system's ability to fight infections.

Simply put, loneliness can kill you.

A basic strategy for happiness, then, is to accept social invitations whenever possible or to initiate social gatherings with family and friends. Psychologists Ed Diener and Martin Seligman found in a 2002 study that the top 10 percent of students with the highest self-reported happiness scores had strong ties to family and friends and committed to spending time with them.[129] So when you get invited to a party, say yes. Schedule date nights with your significant other. Find ways to connect with people.

If you don't have a strong social circle, you'll have to be proactive. Invite coworkers to a drink or to dinner after work on a Friday. Start going to church. Join a book club at your local library. Sign up at the YMCA. If you enjoy exercise, join a running or biking club. Volunteer. Take a class and learn something new alongside other like-minded people. Not only will the social interaction help you, but trying new things will increase the variety in your life and stave off habituation.

Our need for connectedness doesn't end when we go to work. While teachers have social jobs, the happiest ones aren't stuck in their rooms all day, isolated from their colleagues. Teachers who say they collaborate often with other teachers are more likely to report higher levels of job satisfaction and confidence in their ability to teach and to motivate students, according to a 2013 survey of middle-school teachers in 34 countries and regions around the world conducted by the Organization for Economic Co-operation and Development (OECD).[130]

"Those who get to participate and collaborate have a higher feeling of value," said Julie Belanger, an education analyst at the OECD and an author of the 2013 Teaching and Learning International Survey (TALIS).[131] In every country, the teachers who said their profession is valued in society tended also to report that their schools included them in decisions and that there was a positive collaborative atmosphere with other teachers at their school.

"They have the highest job satisfaction and confidence in their teaching abilities," said Belanger. "It's true across the board."[132]

The TALIS report highlighted a number of ways schools can foster collaborative workplaces. Veteran teachers can mentor new teachers. Instead of sending teachers away to workshops for professional development, schools could form networks of teachers and offer professional development in-house. Teachers could collaboratively research shared topics of interest to improve their skills.

Teachers should also be provided with more paid time to work with their colleagues. They can plan units, learn about effective instructional strategies, engage in a whole-school book study, and grade papers collaboratively. On a few occasions, my principal has used meeting time to give teachers the opportunity to score student writing as grade level teams. Our scores were more consistent, and the task was much more enjoyable than having to score them at home, alone, on a Saturday.

Working with others improves happiness and makes teachers, and therefore schools, better. The OECD said that the negative effects of student misbehavior and academic struggles were mitigated in schools where there existed a supportive, collaborative atmosphere to help teachers handle behavioral disruptions.[133]

It's often said that people can work anywhere doing anything as long as they're doing it with people they like. One way for schools to improve the happiness of their teachers is to provide staff with more opportunities to collaborate. And one way for teachers to improve their own happiness is to make sure they're connecting with other people, both inside and outside of school.

21. Manage Your Life

If you're not happy outside of school, you'll find it difficult to be happy inside of school. While there are some for whom work is a refuge, most of us can't compartmentalize well enough to be happy at work if we're depressed at home. To be a happy teacher, it helps to be a happy person.

There are a number of out-of-school factors that will impact your happiness at work. If you don't address them, you'll find it much harder to be a happy teacher. Financial guru Dave Ramsey says that in order to build wealth, you have to tell your money how to behave. If you don't, you won't have any. Your life is the same way. You have to tell your life how to behave. If you don't, you won't have much of one.

Sleep

One of the most important areas of your life to take control of is the amount of sleep you get. We are a nation of sleep-deprived zombies muddling through our days. The CDC reports that 35 percent of Americans regularly get less than seven hours of sleep each night.[134] This has real impacts on nearly every aspect of our lives. A lack of sleep leads to impaired cognitive functions, making us more likely to overreact. We become more irritable, less productive, less creative, and we make worse decisions. We also become fatter, as our tired minds lack the willpower to make good choices and we're too exhausted to even consider exercising. There is even some research that connects sleep deprivation to mental health problems and depression.

After collapsing from exhaustion in 2007, Arianna Huffington became a sleep evangelist. She wrote the book, *The Sleep Revolution: Transforming Your Life One Night at a Time,* and believes that sleep deprivation is the new smoking. She thinks it will soon be viewed by employees as harmful instead of a badge of honor. When told at a forum of a chief executive who is expected to be available 24/7, Huffington replied, "I expect that in two years, you will not be able to make that statement in public."[135] I hope she's right.

Like Huffington, many other high-status people are coming around to the need for more shut eye. Amazon CEO Jeff Bezos now gets eight hours every night. He says, "I'm more alert and I think more clearly. I just feel so much better all day long if I've had eight hours."[136]

Comedian and talk show host Ellen Degeneres told *People* magazine, "I'm usually asleep by 11 p.m. and up around 7:30 a.m. It's a lot!"[137]

Actress Eva Longoria gets eight hours. "Anytime I get less, I pay for it the next day," she explains.[138]

Matthew McConaughey gets eight and a half hours. "I'm not near as good the next day if I get less," he says.[139]

When Warren Buffett started at Salomon Brothers in the early 1990s as an advisor, he told every worker in the New York City office to go home and get a good night's rest.[140]

One way to get enough sleep and to be sure you're refreshed for another day of teaching tomorrow is to leave work at work. Research shows that detachment from work through relaxation and recreation is essential for attention, engagement, and your health. Without recovery from work-related stress, you put yourself at higher risk for heart disease, irritable bowel syndrome, and burnout. You'll also suffer from poorer performance, cynicism, and you'll be absent more often.

Research by Sabine Sonnentag, Charlotte Fritz, and others has shown that a break from the work state of mind allows recovery from strain and ends the pattern of negative feelings that drive pessimism and chronic stress. Studies show that people who are able to detach from the day's work are more likely to report a positive mood in the morning and a reduction in stress, which is critical to increasing your happiness.

According to Sonnentag, detaching means not checking your work email, not taking unfinished business home with you, and forgetting about conflicts you had with students, colleagues, or your principal. Many studies suggest you'll be happier and better at your job if you learn to leave it at school.

Switching off from work leads to higher productivity when you're there. A study in which weekly surveys were collected over the course of four workweeks revealed that when employees detached from their job during the weekend, they felt more refreshed at the beginning of the next workweek and showed more proactive work behavior throughout the week.[141]

Get a Pet

Researcher Allen McConnell has found that social support provided by pets is comparable to that from a family member. Pet owners tend to have greater self-esteem and are less depressed and lonely. They also exercise more.

In one experiment, researchers found that thinking about one's pet countered the negativity that comes from social isolation just as well as thinking about one's best friend.

There is an important caveat. Further observations made by McConnell indicated that the effects of pets on our health and happiness are stronger when we are already have a good social life. After all, having a pet will not change things unless we build a positive relationship with it.[142]

If you're generally happy and like animals, getting a pet may boost your well-being. But if you're lonely and depressed, don't expect a new dog to make everything better.

Exercise

Research suggests that happy people are healthier, but is the reverse true? Are healthy people happier? They seem to think so. According to the Economic Determinants of Happiness, self-described healthy people are 20 percent happier than average, while unhealthy people are 8.25 percent less happy.[143] A major factor for our health is exercise, so it isn't surprising that healthy people report higher levels of happiness. Exercise makes us feel better.

When we exercise, our brains release endorphins, the chemicals known to produce a feeling of euphoria, commonly called the "runner's high." Endorphins trigger the release of hormones that enhance our moods and create a sense of well-being. Exercise also boosts happiness by reducing feelings of stress. When we exercise, our bodies burn the stress hormone cortisol.

Exercise has also been shown to improve the sleep patterns of insomniacs, as well as lower their anxiety. Studies on rats indicate that exercise mimics the effects of antidepressants on the brain. Exercise is also responsible for the creation of new brain cells in the part of the brain responsible for learning and memory.

Exercise increases antibody production by as much as 300 percent. People who exercise also tend to get outside more, which can improve happiness. They put themselves in social environments, such as gyms, running groups, and race events, which gives them the opportunity to connect with people who share similar values and interests. Many exercisers set goals and feel happiness as they make progress toward reaching them. Some benefit from higher self-esteem as a result of losing weight and feeling better about their appearance. They gain confidence, which can create a virtuous cycle, as higher self-esteem leads to more success and more opportunities, which in turn lead to even more confidence, success, and opportunities.

Clearly, exercise is very good for you and good for your happiness. If you'd like some ideas on how to lose weight and start exercising more, you can check out my first book, *The Teacher's Guide to Weight Loss*.

Do Nothing

While connecting with family and friends is vital to your well-being, so is taking the time to do nothing at all. Most people experience a sense of discomfort when they have nothing to do. Walk into any waiting room in America and you won't see anyone just sitting there thinking. They're chatting, or on their phones, or flipping through a magazine. Some people can't even move their bowels without taking something in there to entertain them.

Our best ideas often come when we are idle. How often have you had a great idea in the shower, or driving to work, or while lying in bed? I used to write bad novels, and in the course of telling a story, I'd often get stuck. I couldn't figure out what should happen next. The worst thing I could do was think more about it. Usually, the solution came when I left the work alone and did something mindless. It's hard to come up with great ideas when we're under pressure to do so or when our minds are busy with other matters.

The same thing happens with teaching. I have very few innovative ideas in February. In February, I'm just trying to survive. But in the summer, when my mind is rested and I'm not stressed out from long days in the classroom, I regularly come up with new things to try for the upcoming school year.

Sitting and thinking, instead of always doing, provides teachers with the mental space to be creative. I keep a notebook where I write down things to try in the classroom, and once a month I force myself to just sit and think. Ideas can come from books, blogs, colleagues, social media, or out of left field.

Time to think also allows teachers to reflect on what's working and what isn't. We're all told how important it is to reflect on our lessons. It's part of every teacher evaluation system I know of. But most teachers roll their eyes and think, "Yeah, right. And when am I supposed to do that?"

They ask that question because they don't give themselves permission to do nothing. For most teachers, the thought of their principal walking in and seeing them sitting down and staring off into space is scary. We teachers feel like we must always be doing things, and we fail to realize that thinking counts.

Time to think and reflect lets teachers revisit their vision for the classroom to see if this year's group is still on track or if things have gone off the rails and a recommitment is necessary. Every year, I write down my personal goals and the vision I have for my room. But once in the grip of the day-to-day hustle and bustle, I sometimes find myself just chugging along without thinking about the big things I want my room to be about. Without time to sit and think, I lose track of where I'm supposed to be leading my students.

You may have heard that Google regularly gives its workers 20 percent of their time to let their minds go wandering. Engineers can use this time to pursue pet projects that can benefit Google. It allows for more worker creativity and innovation. They've set up meditation programs and trampolines to offer workers a more imaginative space. Gmail, Adsense, and Google News were all the result of workers being given the time to take a break from their real jobs.

A lot of unenlightened people, possibly including your principal, might look at you askance if they find you sitting at your desk seemingly doing nothing during your planning time. Unfortunately, the value of idleness isn't recognized by everyone. Doing nothing has never really been acceptable. People associate it with irresponsibility. It's seen as a waste of time. In many places, workaholics are highly encouraged, supported, and even rewarded. So if you need to justify your inaction, you can look to famous successful people who value the fine art of doing nothing.

Michael Lewis, the bestselling author of *Moneyball* and *The Big Short*, claims that laziness is the key to his success. He says, "People waste years of their lives not being willing to waste hours of their lives." Laziness prevents him from being overwhelmed with opportunities that he doesn't care about. "My laziness serves as a filter. Something has to be really good before I'll decide to work on it."[144]

Twitter CEO Jack Dorsey takes 30 minutes every morning to meditate, which involves little more than sitting in one place and relaxing. Other meditators include Ford Motor Company Chairman Bill Ford, Oprah Winfrey, hip-hop mogul Russell Simmons, singer Katy Perry, actress Jennifer Aniston, actor Hugh Jackman, movie director David Lynch, and singer Paul McCartney.

J.P. Morgan took two months off every year, explaining, "I can get done in 10 months what I could never do in 12."

Even Ben Franklin, who is often remembered as a workaholic, said, "I am the laziest man in the world. I invented all those things to save myself from toil."

Try New Things

When you're done doing nothing, you should get out into the world and try new things. Variety is indeed the spice of life, and changing things up will increase your happiness. Some people avoid new things because they fear failure or worry about embarrassing themselves. They don't want to risk doing something they will later regret. But research shows that people of every age and every walk of life regret *not* doing things much more than they regret doing things. The most popular regrets people have include not going to college (as opposed to attending and failing), not grasping business opportunities (as opposed to going for it and failing), and not spending enough time with family and friends (as opposed to spending time and regretting it). The reason for this is we find value in our actions even when they end poorly.

I went skiing exactly once in my life. I made the mistake of waiting until I was a teenager. I was terrible. Little kids zipped past and around me. I never figured out how to properly stop, so I just slid like a baseball player all day. I never got off the bunny hill. But I don't regret doing it. I have a fun, if embarrassing, memory of the day. I spent the day with my dad. I learned I didn't like skiing, so I spend winter days doing other stuff now. On the other hand, when I was in college a friend of mine invited me to Hawaii, where his older brother was stationed at the time. It was a great deal. The housing was paid for, so my only expenses would have been the plane ticket and whatever we did for fun. But I didn't go because I was a poor college student. I didn't want to put the ticket on my credit card. It's one of my biggest regrets. I'm 41 and have still never been to Hawaii.

When we try something new and fail, our brains justify our decision. We naturally make the best of it. We console ourselves with the knowledge that we learned a valuable lesson, or that we now have a fantastic story to tell at parties. When we don't do something, our brains can't perform the same trick because there is no lesson be learned and no story to tell.

One new thing you might try is starting or joining an organization that allows you to help others. While teachers sometimes complain they don't have a lot of free time, we do have more discretionary time than many other professionals. With two weeks off at Christmas, a spring break in March or April, and an extended summer vacation, teachers have the opportunity to serve others and make the world a better place.

Stepping outside yourself is a proven way to boost your happiness. Local churches offer numerous opportunities to help. You could volunteer at a soup kitchen or food pantry, provide services to the elderly, work at a summer camp, lead a Girl Scout troop, coach in a summer league, or even use your classroom presentation skills to read to developmentally disabled adults. For more opportunities, check out www.serve.gov.

If you have a particular passion, you can start your own organization. Two years ago, I started Summer Books, an organization that collects old children's books from families who have outgrown them and gives them to at-risk readers in grades K-2. It adds meaning to my life, but it also serves those students who will eventually end up in my classroom. I want them to have every opportunity to love reading and get better at it.

Choose Happiness

Happiness is a choice. A growing body of research provides a roadmap for all of us to follow. Happy teachers make for happy schools, which make for happy students, who will grow up and hopefully become happy adults. A world of happy adults is a world we would all love to be a part of. Take the first steps today toward improving your own happiness, and you will help the world become a better, and much happier, place.

How to Be Happy

Be kind to others
Appreciate everyday moments
Choose a positive attitude
Focus on the good
Be optimistic
Express gratitude
Find meaning in your work
Identify your purpose in life
Give to others
Avoid comparisons
Take control
Have meaningful goals
Make progress toward your goals
Have fun
Smile
Serve
Get recognized
Forgive others
Spend a lot of time with family and friends
Get enough sleep
Have a pet
Relax and think
Try new things
Take care of yourself
Choose to be happy

Final Thoughts

I hope you found this book helpful. I read quite a few inexpensive books like this one, and I always hope I can take away at least one thing that will help me.

If you found anything of value in the book, I have a small favor to ask. Would you please take a few minutes out of your busy day and leave a review on Amazon? Reviews help the message reach other readers, and they help me become a better writer. Thank you.

If you enjoyed the book, you might also like to read my thoughts on the teaching life. You can find more on my website, www.teacherhabits.com. By joining the free subscriber list, you'll get access to downloadable content and also receive email updates whenever I write an article or have a new book coming out. Thank you.

References

To quickly access links to the happiness books below, please visit the Happy Teacher page on my website.

Iggie's House
July Blume

There's a Boy in the Girls' Bathroom
Louis Sachar

The Happiness Equation
Neil Pasricha

Stumbling on Happiness
Daniel Gilbert

The Levity Effect
Adrian Gostick and Scott Christopher

If You're So Smart, Why Aren't You Happy
Raj Raghunathan

Flourish
Martin Seligman

The How of Happiness
Sonja Lyubomirsky

The Worry Trick: How Your Brain Tricks You into Expecting the Worst and What You Can Do About It
David A. Carbonell, PhD

The Happiness Track
Emma Seppälä

The Myths of Happiness
Sonja Lyubomirsky

Happy
Ian K. Smith

Essentialism
Greg McKeown

The Happiness Project
Gretchen Rubin

Best Year Ever
Bill Cecil

Authentic Happiness
Martin Seligman

The Sleep Revolution: Transforming Your Life, One Night at a Time
Arianna Huffington

Acknowledgements

Thanks to the many researchers out there looking into what makes people happy. It's a fascinating field, and I enjoyed reading your work. This book wouldn't be possible without your curiosity and efforts.

Thanks also to my wife, Jeanie, for your understanding. There were days when I spent long hours working on this book, and you never once complained.

Thank you to Dwight Blubaugh, Melissa Nott Schmitz, Paul Ellsworth, and Jeanie Murphy for selflessly giving hours of your time to make this book better. I'm in your debt.

About the Author

Paul Murphy is a third grade teacher in Michigan with 17 years of experience. His writing focuses on improving the lives of teachers, both inside the classroom and out. He enjoys reading, writing, travel, exercise, and Cheetos. His feet are perpetually cold, he bites his nails, and he regularly (and almost instinctively at this point) changes the lyrics to songs to make them inappropriate, much to the chagrin of his wife and daughter.

There are a few good things about him. He does all of his family's grocery shopping, he rarely exceeds his monthly budget, and he's only had two cavities and one speeding ticket in his life.

You can read more at his website, www.teacherhabits.com.

Other Books by Paul Murphy:

The Teacher's Guide to Weight Loss (2017)

Endnotes

1. Hanushek, Eric A. "The Economic Value of Higher Teacher Quality." Economics of Education Review 30.3 (2011): 466-79. Elsevier, 16 Dec. 2010. Web.

2. Gallup, Inc. "Latin Americans Most Positive in the World." Gallup.com. Gallup, 19 Dec. 2012. Web. 02 May 2017.

3. Lyubomirsky, Sonja. The Myths of Happiness: What Should Make You Happy but Doesn't, What Shouldn't Make You Happy but Does. New York: Penguin, 2014. Print.

4. Gallup, Inc. "U.S. Teachers Love Their Lives, but Struggle in the Workplace." Gallup.com. Gallup, 28 Mar. 2013. Web. 02 May 2017.

5. Ibid.

6. Ibid.

7. Ibid.

8. Ibid.

9. "The MetLife Survey of the American Teacher: Challenges for School Leadership (2012)." (2013): n. pag. MetLife, Feb. 2013. Web.

10. Ibid.

11. Gallup, Inc. "U.S. Teachers Love Their Lives, but Struggle in the Workplace." Gallup.com. Gallup, 28 Mar. 2013. Web. 02 May 2017.

12. Richardson, Hannah. "More than 50% of Teachers in England 'plan to Quit in next Two Years'." BBC News. BBC, 04 Oct. 2015. Web.

13. Gallup, Inc. "U.S. Teachers Love Their Lives, but Struggle in the Workplace." Gallup.com. Gallup, 28 Mar. 2013. Web. 02 May 2017.

14. Gray, L., and Taie, S. (2015). Public School Teacher Attrition and Mobility in the First Five Years: Results From the First Through Fifth Waves of the 2007–08 Beginning Teacher Longitudinal Study (NCES 2015-337). U.S. Department of Education. Washington, DC: National Center for Education Statistics.

15. Carroll, Tom, and Kathleen Fulton. "The True Cost of Teacher Turnover." (2004): National Commission on Teaching and America's Future, 2004. Web.

16. Sutcher, L., Darling-Hammond, L., & Carver-Thomas, D. (2016). A coming crisis in teaching? Teacher supply, demand, and shortages in the U.S.. Palo Alto, CA: Learning Policy Institute.

17. "The MetLife Survey of the American Teacher: Challenges for School Leadership (2012)." (2013): n. pag. MetLife, Feb. 2013. Web.

18. Goldhaber, Dan. "National Board Teachers Are More Effective, But Are They in the Classrooms Where They'Re Needed the Most?" Education Finance and Policy, vol. 1, no. 3, 2006, pp. 372–382., www.jstor.org/stable/educfinapoli.1.3.372.

19. Berry, Barnett. Recruiting and Retaining Quality Teachers for High-Needs Schools: Insights from NBCT Summits and Other Policy Initiatives. N.p.: Center for Teaching Quality, n.d. 4. Web.

20. "The MetLife Survey of the American Teacher: Challenges for School Leadership (2012)." (2013): n. pag. MetLife, Feb. 2013. Web.

21. Pasricha, Neil. The Happiness Equation: Want Nothing Do Anything = Have Everything. London: Vermilion, 2017. Print.

22. White, Mary. "Which Professionals Are Prone to Burnout?" LoveToKnow. LoveToKnow Corp, n.d. Web. 02 May 2017. <http://stress.lovetoknow.com/Which_Professionals_are_Prone_to _Burnout>.

23. Berry, Barnett. Recruiting and Retaining Quality Teachers for High-Needs Schools: Insights from NBCT Summits and Other Policy Initiatives. N.p.: Center for Teaching Quality, n.d. 5. Web.

24. Gilbert, Daniel Todd. Stumbling on Happiness. New York: A.A. Knopf, 2006. Print.

25. Ibid.

26. Kahneman, D., and A. Deaton. "High Income Improves Evaluation of Life but Not Emotional Well-being." Proceedings of the National Academy of Sciences 107.38 (2010): 16489-6493. Web.

27. Brickman, P., R. Janoff-Bulman, and D. Coates. Lottery Winners and Accident Victims: Is Happiness Relative? 8th ed. Vol. 36. N.p.: Journal of Personality and Social Psychology, 1978. 917-927. Web.

28. Stewart-Brown, S., P. C. Samaraweera, F. Taggart, N.-B. Kandala, and S. Stranges. "Socioeconomic Gradients and Mental Health: Implications for Public Health." The British Journal of Psychiatry 206.6 (2015): 461-65. Web.

29. Thomas, Michael L., Christopher N. Kaufmann, Barton W. Palmer, Colin A. Depp, Averria Sirkin Martin, Danielle K. Glorioso, Wesley K. Thompson, and Dilip V. Jeste. "Paradoxical Trend for Improvement in Mental Health With Aging." The Journal of Clinical Psychiatry(2016): n. pag. Web.

30. Kahneman, D. "A Survey Method for Characterizing Daily Life Experience: The Day Reconstruction Method." Science 306.5702 (2004): 1776-780. Web.

31. Wallace, David Foster. This Is Water Some Thoughts, Delivered on a Significant Occasion about Living a Compassionate Life. Boston: Little, Brown and Company, 2009. Print.

32. Thompson, Derek. "What Is the Secret to Happiness and Money?" The Atlantic. Atlantic Media Company, 23 Mar. 2011. Web. 02 May 2017. <https://www.theatlantic.com/business/archive/2011/03/what-is-the-secret-to-happiness-and-money/72874/>.

33. Ferrari, Eva, and J. Freeman. "The Power of Nice: A Study Exploring the Relationship between Participant Ratings of How 'nice' They Are, Their Behaviour, and Their Reported Levels of Health, Happiness and Success." I2 Media Research Limited (2017): n. pag. Print.

34. Linsin, Michael. The Happy Teacher Habits. Kindle version. Retrieved from www.amazon.com.

35. Crotty, James Marshall. "Allen Iverson Earned Over $200 Million In His NBA Career. Now He's Reportedly Broke. Say, What?" Forbes. Forbes Magazine, 12 Nov. 2012. Web. <https://www.forbes.com/sites/jamesmarshallcrotty/2012/02/21/allen-iverson-earned-over-200-million-in-his-nba-career-hes-now-broke-say-what/#439bcb3e34fe>.

36. Glauber, Bill. "Teacher Who Won Powerball Millions in 1993 Runs Camp for Kids." Teacher Who Won Powerball Millions in 1993 Runs Camp for Kids. Milwaukee Journal Sentinel, 3 Aug. 2009. Web. <http://archive.jsonline.com/news/wisconsin/54185307.html>.

37. Cheung, Sam. "Lottery Winner Craig Henshaw Paid a Big Price for His Millions." Thestar.com. 08 May 2012. Web. <https://www.thestar.com/news/gta/2012/05/08/lottery_winner_craig_henshaw_paid_a_big_price_for_his_millions.html>.

38. "2012-2013 Average Starting Teacher Salaries by State." NEA. 2013. Web. <http://www.nea.org/home/2012-2013-average-starting-teacher-salary.html>.

39. "Salary: Teacher." Glassdoor. N.p., 25 Apr. 2017. Web. <https://www.glassdoor.com/Salaries/teacher-salary-SRCH_KO0,7.htm>.

40. Behavior, Modeled. "The Data Shows Teachers Are Still Highly Respected." Forbes. Forbes Magazine, 14 June 2014. Web. <https://www.forbes.com/sites/modeledbehavior/2014/06/14/teachers-highly-respected/#7e8bf8014555>.

41. "Honesty/Ethics in Professions." Gallup.com. Gallup, Inc., 19 Dec. 2016. Web. <http://www.gallup.com/poll/1654/honesty-ethics-professions.aspx>.

42. Fuller, Ed. "Examining Principal Turnover." Shanker Institute, 23 Feb. 2015. Web. <http://www.shankerinstitute.org/blog/examining-principal-turnover>.

43. Kim, E., K. Hagan, F. Grodstein, D. DeMeo, I. De Vito, and L.

Kubzansky. "Optimism and Cause-Specific Mortality: A Prospective Cohort Study." American Journal of Epidemiology 185.1 (2017): n. pag. Web.

44. Publications, Harvard Health. "Optimism and Your Health." Harvard Health. N.p., May 2008. Web. <http://www.health.harvard.edu/heart-health/optimism-and-your-health>.

45. Simon-Thomas, E. R., and J. A. Smith. "How Grateful Are Americans?" Greater Good. N.p., 10 Jan. 2013. Web. <http://greatergood.berkeley.edu/article/item/how_grateful_are_am ericans>.

46. Cecil, Bill. Best Year Ever!: Winning Strategies to Thrive in Today's Classroom. Wheaton, IL: Best Year Ever!, 2007. Print.

47. Seligman, Martin E. P. Flourish. North Sydney, NSW: Random House Australia, 2012. Print.

48. "Are Religious People Happier People?" The Austin Institute for the Study of Family and Culture, 2014. Web. <http://relationshipsinamerica.com/religion/are-religious-people-happier-people>.

49. Mitchell, Travis. "Religion in Everyday Life." Pew Research Center's Religion & Public Life Project. N.p., 12 Apr. 2016. Web. <http://www.pewforum.org/2016/04/12/religion-in-everyday-life/>.

50. Lim, Chaeyoon, and Robert D. Putnam. "Religion, Social Networks, and Life Satisfaction."American Sociological Review 75.6 (2010): 914-33. Web.

51. Putnam, Robert D., David E. Campbell, and Shaylyn Romney. Garrett. American Grace: How Religion Divides and Unites Us. New York: Simon & Schuster, 2012. Print.

52. "Who Mentored You." Harvard T.H. Chan School of Public Health, n.d. Web. <https://sites.sph.harvard.edu/wmy/celebrities/president-bill-clinton/>.

53. Serwer, Interview By Andy. "Best Advice From Bill Gates and Bill

Gates Sr." Best Advice from Bill Gates and Bill Gates Sr. - Jun. 21,
2009. N.p., 21 June 2009. Web.
<http://archive.fortune.com/2009/06/18/magazines/fortune/best_ad
vice_bill_gates.fortune/index.htm>.

54. "Myths and Facts about Educator Pay." NEA. N.p., n.d. Web.
<http://www.nea.org/home/12661.htm>.

55. Dunn, Elizabeth W., Lara B. Aknin, and Michael I. Norton.
"Prosocial Spending and Happiness: Using Money to Benefit
Others Pays Off." Current Directions in Psychological Science.
https://dash.harvard.edu/handle/1/11189976. Web.

56. Ibid.

57. Aknin, Lara B., J. Kiley Hamlin, and Elizabeth W. Dunn. "Giving
Leads to Happiness in Young Children." PLoS ONE 7.6 (2012): n.
pag. Web.

58. Silver, Nate. "Do Americans Really Hate Flying? Or Really Love
Driving?" FiveThirtyEight, 07 May 2014. Web.
<https://fivethirtyeight.com/features/do-americans-really-hate-flying-
or/>.

59. Lyubomirsky, Sonja. The Myths of Happiness: What Should Make
You Happy but Doesn't, What Shouldn't Make You Happy but
Does. New York: Penguin, 2014. Print.

60. Lyubomirsky, Sonja. The Myths of Happiness: What Should Make
You Happy but Doesn't, What Shouldn't Make You Happy but
Does. New York: Penguin, 2014. Print.

61. Robbins, R., and K. Trzesniewski. "Self-Esteem Across the
Lifespan." Current Directions in Psychological Science (2005): n.
pag. Web.
<http://www.psy.miami.edu/faculty/dmessinger/c_c/rsrcs/rdgs/emot/
robins_trz.selfesteemdevel_curidr2005.pdf>.

62. Baker David A. and Algorta Guillermo Perez. Cyberpsychology,
Behavior, and Social Networking. November 2016, 19(11): 638-
648. doi:10.1089/cyber.2016.0206.

63. Vogel, Erin A., Jason P. Rose, Lindsay R. Roberts, and Katheryn Eckles. "Social Comparison, Social Media, and Self-esteem." Psychology of Popular Media Culture 3.4 (2014): 206-22. Web.

64. Tromholt Morten. Cyberpsychology, Behavior, and Social Networking. November 2016, 19(11): 661-666. doi:10.1089/cyber.2016.0259.

65. "Emotional Health Higher Among Older Americans." Gallup.com. Gallup, Inc., 12 Aug. 2011. Web. <http://www.gallup.com/poll/148994/Emotional-Health-Higher-Among-Older-Americans.aspx?utm_source=alert&utm_medium=email&utm_campaign=syndication&utm_content=morelink&utm_term=All%2BGallup%2BHeadlines%2B-%2BWellbeing>.

66. "Self-determination Theory." Wikipedia. Wikimedia Foundation, 24 Mar. 2017. Web. <https://en.wikipedia.org/wiki/Self-determination_theory#Needs>.

67. "Illusion of Control." Wikipedia. Wikimedia Foundation, 09 Apr. 2017. Web. <https://en.wikipedia.org/wiki/Illusion_of_control>.

68. LeBeau, Phil. "Drivers Aren't Ready to Hand over Control Just Yet." CNBC. CNBC, 16 July 2015. Web. <http://www.cnbc.com/2015/07/16/drivers-arent-ready-to-give-up-control-just-yet.html>.

69. Sparks, D., and N. Malkus. "Public School Teacher Autonomy in the Classroom Across School Years 2003–04, 2007–08, and 2011–12." U.S. Department of Education (2015): n. pag. Web. <https://nces.ed.gov/pubs2015/2015089.pdf>.

70. Ibid.

71. "Teacher Autonomy Declined Over Past Decade, New Data Shows." NEA Today. N.p., 27 Jan. 2016. Web. <http://neatoday.org/2016/01/11/teacher-autonomy-in-the-classroom/>.

72. Riggs, Liz. "Why Do Teachers Quit?" The Atlantic. Atlantic Media Company, 18 Oct. 2013. Web.

<https://www.theatlantic.com/education/archive/2013/10/why-do-teachers-quit/280699/>.

73. Trosclair, Alice. "Why Teachers Leave - and Possible Solutions." The Educators Room. Washington Post, 01 Nov. 2016. Web. <http://theeducatorsroom.com/2015/06/teachers-leave-possible-solutions/>.

74. Kuster, Elizabeth. "5 Things Every Happy Person Does." The Huffington Post. TheHuffingtonPost.com, 12 Oct. 2012. Web. <http://www.huffingtonpost.com/2012/10/12/happy-people-joy-happiness_n_1927088.html>.

75. Kuster, Elizabeth. "5 Things Every Happy Person Does." The Huffington Post. TheHuffingtonPost.com, 12 Oct. 2012. Web. <http://www.huffingtonpost.com/2012/10/12/happy-people-joy-happiness_n_1927088.html>.

76. "BBC - Press Office - Jonathan Ross Meets JK Rowling." BBC News. BBC, 7 June 2007. Web. <http://www.bbc.co.uk/pressoffice/pressreleases/stories/2007/07_july/06/ross.shtml>.

77. Kramer, Teresa AmabileSteven J. "The Power of Small Wins." Harvard Business Review. N.p., 08 June 2016. Web. <https://hbr.org/2011/05/the-power-of-small-wins>.

78. Davidson, Richard J. Anxiety, Depression, and Emotion. Oxford: Oxford UP, 2011. 91-92. Print.

79. Stambor, Zak. "How Laughing Leads to Learning." PsycEXTRA Dataset 37.6 (2006): n. pag. Web.

80. Sgroi, D. "Happiness and Productivity: Understanding the Happy-productive Worker." Social Market Foundation (2015): n. pag. Web. <http://www.smf.co.uk/wp-content/uploads/2015/10/Social-Market-Foundation-Publication-Briefing-CAGE-4-Are-happy-workers-more-productive-281015.pdf>.

81. Sieler, B. "School of Medicine Study Shows Laughter Helps Blood Vessels Function Better."University of Maryland Medical Center (2005): n. pag. Web. <http://www.umm.edu/news-and-events/news-

releases/2005/school-of-medicine-study-shows-laughter-helps-blood-vessels-function-better>.

82. Gostick, Adrian Robert., and Scott Christopher. The Levity Effect: Why It Pays to Lighten up. Hoboken, NJ: John Wiley & Sons, 2008. Print..

83. "Fortune 100 Best Companies to Work For 2017." Great Place To Work United States. N.p., 2017. Web. <https://www.greatplacetowork.com/best-workplaces/100-best/2017>.

84. Gostick, Adrian Robert., and Scott Christopher. The Levity Effect: Why It Pays to Lighten up. Hoboken, NJ: John Wiley & Sons, 2008. Print. 14.

85. Gostick, Adrian Robert., and Scott Christopher. The Levity Effect: Why It Pays to Lighten up. Hoboken, NJ: John Wiley & Sons, 2008. Print. 21-22.

86. Gostick, Adrian Robert., and Scott Christopher. The Levity Effect: Why It Pays to Lighten up. Hoboken, NJ: John Wiley & Sons, 2008. Print. 11-12

87. Darrentyler. "Louis CK Everything Is Amazing And Nobody Is Happy." YouTube. YouTube, 24 Oct. 2015. Web. <https://www.youtube.com/watch?v=q8LaT5Iiwo4>.

88. Nawijn, Jeroen, Miquelle A. Marchand, Ruut Veenhoven, and Ad J. Vingerhoets. "Vacationers Happier, but Most Not Happier After a Holiday." Applied Research in Quality of Life 5.1 (2010): 35-47. Web.

89. Jaffe, Eric. "The Psychological Study of Smiling." Association for Psychological Science. N.p., Dec. 2010. Web. <https://www.psychologicalscience.org/observer/the-psychological-study-of-smiling#.WQk5PPQrLrc>.

90. Harker, Leeanne, and Dacher Keltner. "Expressions of Positive Emotion in Women's College Yearbook Pictures and Their Relationship to Personality and Life Outcomes across Adulthood." Journal of Personality and Social Psychology 80.1 (2001): 112-24.

Web.

91. Abel, Ernest L., and Michael L. Kruger. "Smile Intensity in Photographs Predicts Longevity."Psychological Science 21.4 (2010): 542-44. Web.

92. Strack, Fritz, Leonard L. Martin, and Sabine Stepper. "Inhibiting and Facilitating Conditions of the Human Smile: A Nonobtrusive Test of the Facial Feedback Hypothesis." Journal of Personality and Social Psychology 54.5 (1988): 768-77. Web.

93. Kraft, Tara L., and Sarah D. Pressman. "Grin and Bear It." Psychological Science 23.11 (2012): 1372-378. Web.

94. Fowler, J. H., and N. A. Christakis. "Dynamic Spread of Happiness in a Large Social Network: Longitudinal Analysis over 20 Years in the Framingham Heart Study." Bmj 337.Dec04 2 (2008): n. pag. Web.

95. Aubrey, A. "Happiness: It Really Is Contagious." NPR. NPR, 2009. Web. <http://www.npr.org/templates/text/s.php?sId=97831171&m=1>.

96. Goldhaber, D. "The Mystery of Good Teaching." Education Next. N.p., 06 July 2011. Web. <http://educationnext.org/the-mystery-of-good-teaching/>.

97. Conradt, S. "11 of the Best Customer Service Stories Ever." Mental Floss. N.p., 15 Dec. 2015. Web. <http://mentalfloss.com/article/30198/11-best-customer-service-stories-ever>.

98. Hsieh, Tony. "How I Did It: Zappos's CEO on Going to Extremes for Customers." Harvard Business Review. N.p., 31 July 2014. Web. <https://hbr.org/2010/07/how-i-did-it-zapposs-ceo-on-going-to-extremes-for-customers>.

99. Ibid.

100. Seligman, Martin E. P. Flourish. North Sydney, NSW: Random House Australia, 2012. Print, 20

101. Luks, Allan, "Doing Good: Helper's High," Psychology Today 22, no. 10 (1988)

102. Oman, Doug, Carl E. Thoresen, and Kay Mcmahon. "Volunteerism and Mortality among the Community-dwelling Elderly." Journal of Health Psychology 4.3 (1999): 301-16. Web.

103. Rees, Michael A., Jonathan E. Kopke, Ronald P. Pelletier, Dorry L. Segev, Matthew E. Rutter, Alfredo J. Fabrega, Jeffrey Rogers, Oleh G. Pankewycz, Janet Hiller, Alvin E. Roth, Tuomas Sandholm, M. Utku Ãnver, and Robert A. Montgomery. "A Nonsimultaneous, Extended, Altruistic-Donor Chain." New England Journal of Medicine 360.11 (2009): 1096-101. Web.

104. Otake, Keiko, Satoshi Shimai, JUNKO TANAKA-MATSUMI, Kanako Otsui, and BARBARA L. FREDRICKSON. "HAPPY PEOPLE BECOME HAPPIER THROUGH KINDNESS: A COUNTING KINDNESSES INTERVENTION." Journal of Happiness Studies. U.S. National Library of Medicine, Sept. 2006. Web. <https://www.ncbi.nlm.nih.gov/pmc/articles/PMC1820947/>.

105. "The Wizard of Electricity." T.P.'s Weekly 10.264 (107): 695. Web.

106. Canfield, Jack, and Mark Victor. Hansen. Chicken Soup for the Teacher's Soul: Stories to Open the Heart and Rekindle the Spirit of Educators. Deerfield Beach, FL: Health Communications, 2002. Print.

107. Kruse, Kevin. "Leadership Secrets From Yum! Brands CEO David Novak." Forbes. Forbes Magazine, 26 June 2014. Web. <https://www.forbes.com/sites/kevinkruse/2014/06/25/david-novack-leadership-advice/#67437a3c7a35>.

108. Commentary. "The Man Who Ran Yum! Brands for 14 Years Has a Simple Way to Judge a Company." Quartz. Quartz, 11 Sept. 2016. Web. <https://qz.com/777101/yum-brands-former-ceo-david-novak-on-the-one-thing-that-makes-companies-successful/>.

109. "The Power of Praise and Recognition." Gallup.com. Gallup, Inc., 08 July 2004. Web. <http://www.gallup.com/businessjournal/12157/power-praise-recognition.aspx>.

110. Ibid.

111. "Ways to Recognize Teachers During Teacher Appreciation Week and All Year Long." The Glenville Democrat, 7 May 2015.

112. "Press Release Details." Bersin by Deloitte. Bersin & Associates, 12 June 2012. Web. <http://www.bersin.com/News/Content.aspx?id=15543>.

113. Novak, David. "Recognizing Employees Is the Simplest Way to Improve Morale." Harvard Business Review. N.p., 09 May 2016. Web. <https://hbr.org/2016/05/recognizing-employees-is-the-simplest-way-to-improve-morale>.

114. Ibid.

115. Ibid.

116. "The Guide to Modern Employee Recognition 17 Unique Examples of Employee Recognition in Action." 17 Unique Examples of Employee Recognition in Action. Bonusly, n.d. Web. <https://bonus.ly/employee-recognition-guide/employee-recognition-examples>.

117. Keating, Caitlin. "Ady Guzman-DeJesus Forgives Daughter's Killer, Helps Him Get a Lighter Sentence." PEOPLE.com. Time Inc, 12 June 2014. Web. <http://people.com/human-interest/ady-guzman-dejesus-forgives-daughters-killer-helps-him-get-a-lighter-sentence/>.

118. Enright, R.D., & Coyle, C.T. (1998). Researching the process model of forgiveness within psychological interventions. In E.L. Worthington, Jr. (Ed.), Dimensions of forgiveness (pp. 139-161). Philadelphia: Templeton Foundation Press.

119. Witvliet, Charlotte Van Oyen, Thomas E. Ludwig, and Kelly L. Vander Laan. "Granting Forgiveness or Harboring Grudges: Implications for Emotion, Physiology, and Health."Psychological Science 12.2 (2001): 117-23. Web.

120. Toussaint, Loren L.; Williams, David R.; Musick, Marc A.; Everson, Susan A.; (2001). "Forgiveness and Health: Age

Differences in a U.S. Probability Sample." Journal of Adult Development 8(4): 249-257. <http://hdl.handle.net/2027.42/44638>

121. Ovalledovalle@miamiherald.com, David. "Miami Teen Who Accidentally Shot Classmate Joins Victim's Mom in Talk to Students." Miami Herald. N.p., 9 Feb. 2016. Web. <http://www.miamiherald.com/news/local/community/miami-dade/homestead/article59381108.html>.

122. Kahneman, D. "A Survey Method for Characterizing Daily Life Experience: The Day Reconstruction Method." Science 306.5702 (2004): 1776-780. Web.

123. Burke, Moira, and Robert E. Kraut. "The Relationship Between Facebook Use and Well-Being Depends on Communication Type and Tie Strength." Journal of Computer-Mediated Communication 21.4 (2016): 265-81. Web.

124. Penenberg, Adam L. "Social Networking Affects Brains Like Falling in Love." Fast Company. Fast Company, 04 Aug. 2012. Web. <https://www.fastcompany.com/1659062/social-networking-affects-brains-falling-love>.

125. Kundu, Mohini. "Science Says You CAN Pinpoint The Source Of Happiness.. And It's Not What Most People Think (VIDEO)." The Huffington Post. TheHuffingtonPost.com, 06 Jan. 2014. Web. <http://www.huffingtonpost.com/2014/01/06/tpl-what-makes-people-happy_n_4548604.html>.

126. Kross, E., M. G. Berman, W. Mischel, E. E. Smith, and T. D. Wager. "Social Rejection Shares Somatosensory Representations with Physical Pain." Proceedings of the National Academy of Sciences 108.15 (2011): 6270-275. Web.

127. Mcpherson, Miller, Lynn Smith-Lovin, and Matthew E. Brashears. "Social Isolation in America: Changes in Core Discussion Networks over Two Decades." American Sociological Review 71.3 (2006): 353-75. Web.

128. San Diego State University. "Depression increasing across the United States." ScienceDaily. ScienceDaily, 30 September 2014. <www.sciencedaily.com/releases/2014/09/140930132832.htm>.

129. Diener, Ed, and Martin E.p. Seligman. "Very Happy People." Psychological Science 13.1 (2002): 81-84. Web.

130. "The OECD Teaching and Learning International Survey (TALIS) - 2013 Results." The OECD Teaching and Learning International Survey (TALIS) - 2013 Results - OECD. N.p., 2013. Web. <http://www.oecd.org/edu/school/talis-2013-results.htm>.

131. Barshay, J. "What Makes for Happier Teachers, According to International Survey."Education By The Numbers. The Hechinger Report, 30 June 2014. Web. <http://educationbythenumbers.org/content/teachers-top-performing-countries-teach-less_1404/>.

132. Ibid.

133. "The OECD Teaching and Learning International Survey (TALIS) - 2013 Results." The OECD Teaching and Learning International Survey (TALIS) - 2013 Results - OECD. N.p., 2013. Web. <http://www.oecd.org/edu/school/talis-2013-results.htm>.

134. "1 in 3 Adults Don't Get Enough Sleep." Centers for Disease Control and Prevention. Centers for Disease Control and Prevention, n.d. Web. <https://www.cdc.gov/media/releases/2016/p0215-enough-sleep.html>.

135. Mullany, Anjali. "Here's Arianna Huffington's Recipe For A Great Night Of Sleep." Fast Company. Fast Company, 02 May 2017. Web. <https://www.fastcompany.com/3060801/heres-arianna-huffingtons-recipe-for-a-great-night-of-sleep>.

136. Jeffrey, Nancy. "Sleep Is the New Status Symbol For Successful Entrepreneurs." The Wall Street Journal. Dow Jones & Company, 02 Apr. 1999. Web. <https://www.wsj.com/news/articles/SB923008887262090895>.

137. Staff, People. "How Much Beauty Sleep Do You Get? – Vol. 75 No. 16." PEOPLE.com. Time Inc, 25 Apr. 2011. Web. <http://people.com/archive/how-much-beauty-sleep-do-you-get-vol-75-no-16/>.

138. Ibid.

139. Ibid.

140. McCarthy, K. "Get Some Sleep and Grow Rich." Ken McCarthy Internet Marketing and beyond. N.p., n.d. Web. <http://kenmccarthy.com/blog/sleep-and-grow-rich>.

141. Sonnentag, Sabine. "Psychological Detachment From Work During Leisure Time." Current Directions in Psychological Science 21.2 (2012): 114-18. Web.

142. Mcconnell, Allen R., Christina M. Brown, Tonya M. Shoda, Colleen M. Martin, and Laura E. Stayton. "Friends with Benefits: On the Positive Consequences of Pet Ownership."PsycEXTRA Dataset 101.6 (2011): n. pag. Web.

143. Guo, Teng, and Lingyi Hu. "Economic Determinants of Happiness." [1112.5802] Economic Determinants of Happiness. N.p., 25 Dec. 2011. Web. <https://arxiv.org/abs/1112.5802>.

144. Zetlin, Minda. "Being Lazy Is the Key to Success, According to the Best-Selling Author of 'Moneyball'." Inc.com. Inc., 20 Mar. 2017. Web. <https://www.inc.com/minda-zetlin/why-being-lazy-makes-you-successful-according-to-the-bestselling-author-of-money.html>.

Made in the USA
Middletown, DE
13 January 2020